BY MARK CUBBEDGE

TEHABI
sports

The Ultimate PGA TOUR Book of Trivia was developed and published by Tehabi Sports, an imprint of Tehabi Books, Inc. Tehabi is the official book publishing licensee of the PGA TOUR and has produced and published many award-winning sports and other non-fiction books that are recognized for their strong literary and visual content. Tehabi works with national and international brands, corporations, institutions, and nonprofit groups to identify, develop, and implement comprehensive publishing programs. Tehabi Books is located in San Diego, California. www.tehabi.com

President and Publisher: Chris Capen
Senior Vice President: Sam Lewis
Vice President and Creative Director: Karla Olson
Director, PGA TOUR Publishing Program:
Marci Weinberg
Director, Corporate Publishing: Chris Brimble
Manager, Corporate Sales: Andrew Arias

Senior Art Director: Charles McStravick
Production Artist: Monika Stout
Illustrator: Scrojo
Editor: Betsy Holt
Editorial Assistant: Emily Henning
Copy Editor: Lisa Wolff
Indexer: Dawn Mayeda

Special thanks to key individuals at the PGA TOUR for their invaluable contributions to The Ultimate PGA TOUR Book of Trivia: Donna Orender, Senior Vice President, Strategic Development; Robert J. Combs, Senior Vice President, Public Relations and Communications; Kirsten Sabia, Director, Brand Integration; Ward Clayton, Director, Editorial Services; Laury Livsey, Manager of Corporate Communications; and Maureen Feeley, Publications Assistant. And special thanks to Bob Rosen and Jennifer Unter of RLR Associates.

ISBN-13: 978-1-933208-03-9
ISBN-10: 1-933208-03-1

Library of Congress Cataloging-in-Publication Data

Cubbedge, Mark.
   The ultimate PGA tour book of trivia / by Mark Cubbedge.
      p. cm.
   ISBN 1-933208-03-1 (pbk. : alk. paper)
   1. Golf–Miscellanea. 2. PGA Tour (Association)–Miscellanea I. PGA Tour (Association) II. Title.
   GV967+

                    2005000034

Tehabi Books offers special discounts for bulk purchases of The Ultimate PGA TOUR Book of Trivia. Copies may be used for corporate hospitality, sales promotions, and/or premium items. Specific needs can be met with customized covers, letter inserts, single-copy mailing cartons with a corporate imprint, and the repurposing of materials into new editions. For more information, contact Andrew Arias, Corporate Sales Manager, Tehabi Books, 4920 Carroll Canyon Road, Suite 200, San Diego, California 92121-3735; 1-800-243-7259.

In the United States, trade bookstores and other book retailers may contact Publishers Group West for sales and distribution information at 1-800-788-3123. Specialty golf retailers may contact The Booklegger for sales and distribution information at 1-800-262-1556.

In Canada, The Ultimate PGA TOUR Book of Trivia is distributed by Georgetown Publications, Inc., 34 Armstrong Avenue, Georgetown, ON L7G 4R9 CANADA; 1-888-595-3008.

Printed in Verona, Italy, by Editoriale Bortolazzi-Stei. Tehabi is proud to partner with EBS in the printing and binding of this and other titles in the PGA TOUR Publishing Program.
Printed on 100gsm Gardamatt.

10 9 8 7 6 5 4 3 2 1

THE ULTIMATE
PGA TOUR
BOOK OF TRIVIA

CONTENTS

The Ultimate PGA TOUR Book of Trivia comes directly from the experts–the people who know the game of golf inside and out, and have witnessed the greatest moments and greatest players from the other side of the ropes. Here you'll find more than 600 interactive questions and answers that cover everything from early golf history to the latest record-breaking feats of the PGA TOUR's favorite golfers.

To find the sport's best, most bizarre brain-teasers, we combed through manuscripts and documents dating back hundreds of years. We dusted off the official USGA rulebooks, broke open the PGA TOUR record books, and even probed the minds of the planet's top players–including members of the World Golf Hall of Fame. The result is a unique collection of humorous anecdotes and personal information about many of golf's greats, as well as hard-core statistics, rules, and facts about the game. Even if you never get through Q-school to get your TOUR card, you can always brush up on your trivia game. So go ahead, tee off–put your golf knowledge to the test!

– MARK CUBBEDGE –

INTRODUCTION

THE GAME

Birdies in Paradise

**Don't play too much golf.
Two rounds a day are plenty.**

– HARRY VARDON –

1
Why was Ed Oliver disqualified from the 1940 U.S. Open?

2
Standing at the second tee leading the 2001 British Open, Ian Woosnam discovered he had 15 clubs in his bag. What was his penalty?

3
Your ball lands near a tree on the edge of the greens, so you bend back the branches in order to get a better shot. What rule have you broken?

4
Which of the following is true about playing from a waste bunker?
A) You can ground your club.
B) You can remove loose impediments.
C) You must rake it entirely after playing from it.
D) Both A and B

5
You accidentally breach the rules during the playoff of a stroke-play competition and are disqualified. Are you disqualified from the competition or just from the playoff round?

1. *He was in a rush to complete his round before a storm set in, so he teed off before his tee time and was consequently disqualified. Oliver would have tied for first if it weren't for his mistake.*

2. *The penalty for carrying more than 14 clubs is two strokes per hole, with a maximum of four strokes per round. Since Woosnam had not yet played the second hole, he was penalized two strokes, knocking him out of the lead and costing him a shot at golf's oldest championship.*

3. *Rule 13-2, which states that you cannot bend or break anything fixed or growing that will improve your lie, stance, or area of intended swing*

4. *D) Both A and B are correct.*

5. *Just from the playoff round. The disqualification only applies to the playoff since it is considered a new stipulated round.*

6

Which of the following is not considered a loose impediment?
A) Pinecones   B) Animal droppings
C) Soda cans   D) Twigs

7

True or false: You should repair any damage to a green made by the impact of your ball, but damage left by players in a previous group can be left for the grounds crew to repair.

8

During a 1987 event Craig Stadler had to play a shot from under a low-hanging tree branch, which required him to play from his knees. To keep his pants from getting wet, he laid down a towel. What rule did he inadvertently break?

9

What criterion does Tiger Woods, winner of more than 40 PGA TOUR events and eight majors, still need to meet in order to qualify for the World Golf Hall of Fame?

10

What is the governing body for golf outside the United States and Mexico?

11

Which of the four major championships has been contested in both stroke play and match play formats?

6 C) Soda cans. Loose impediments are defined as naturally occurring objects and are considered part of the course.

7 False. Proper golf etiquette states that players should repair any damage made by golf balls, whether or not the damage is from their ball.

8 Rule 13-3, which states that a player cannot build a stance. Breaking this rule results in a two-stroke penalty.

9 He needs to reach his 40th birthday, which is the minimum age for eligibility.

10 The Royal and Ancient Golf Club of St. Andrews

11 The PGA Championship was a match play competition from 1916 to 1957 before turning to the stroke play format in 1958.

12

During what competition format would you likely hear the greenside announcement, "Davis Love III concedes Colin Montgomerie's par putt to halve the hole. The players are all square"?

13

Two players, teamed against two others, each play their ball through a hole, but mark down only the best score of the two balls on their team. What format is this?

14

Prior to the 2004 Ryder Cup, Phil Mickelson practiced with the same type of ball Tiger Woods uses in competition. Why?

15

Darren Clarke and Jerry Kelly halved the 14th hole at the 2004 World Golf Championships–Accenture Match Play Championship, making Clarke 4-up with four holes to play. What official golf term describes this situation?

16

What is the origin of the word "fore"?

17

From what does the term "mulligan" derive?

18

During stroke play, which ball is played first?
A) The ball nearest the hole
B) The ball farthest from the hole
C) The balls in the fairway
D) The balls outside the fairway

12 *Match play, which is used in The Presidents Cup, the Ryder Cup, and a World Golf Championships event on the PGA TOUR*

13 *Four-ball, where the format is best-ball scoring*

14 *The two were going to be paired in foursomes play, which requires players to alternate hitting the same ball. Mickelson, who played a different ball than Woods, was getting familiar with the feel of another ball.*

15 *The match play term "dormie," which means that one side is up by the same number of holes that remain to be played.*

16 *The term evolved from the 19th-century word "forecaddie," a person who walked ahead of golfers and helped locate errant balls.*

17 *According to the USGA, the most widely accepted origin is credited to Canadian David Mulligan, who re-teed a shot at the St. Lambert Country Club in Montreal, Quebec, in the 1920s.*

18 *B) The ball farthest from the hole*

19

Approximately how many rounds
of golf were played in 2003?
A) 100 million   B) 200 million
C) 500 million   D) 1 billion

20

Which states have the most
golf courses (in descending order)?
A) Florida, California, Michigan, and Texas
B) Florida, California, Texas, and Michigan
C) California, Florida, Michigan, and Texas
D) California, Florida, Texas, and New York

21

What five states are the most
popular destinations for golfers?

22

What percentage of golfers
regularly score better than 90 on a
regulation-length, 18-hole course?

23

How many scores have to be posted before
a handicap index can be issued to a player?
A) 5 B) 10 C) 15 D) 20

24

True or false: The USGA
issues handicaps to golfers.

25

What handicap does
George W. Bush carry?
A) 5   B) 10   C) 15
D) 20 or higher

19 *C) Almost 500 million*

20 *A) Florida (1,073 courses), California (912 courses), Michigan (854 courses), and Texas (838 courses), according to the National Golf Foundation's 2003 records*

21 *Florida, South Carolina, North Carolina, California, and Arizona*

22 *22 percent*

23 *A) 5*

24 *False. The USGA develops the handicap formula, but actual handicaps are issued through the individual clubs.*

25 *C) 15*

26 ▶

Arnold Palmer made two holes-in-one at the same hole–on
successive days–in a two-day pro-am before the 1986 Chrysler Cup.
Graham Marsh had a similar feat at the 2004 Senior British Open,
making aces at No. 11 during the first and third rounds. What are
the odds of an average player even making one hole-in-one?

27 ▶

During the 2001 Buick Invitational playoff, Phil Mickelson and Frank Lickliter
both hit provisional tee shots into a ravine on the third hole. Both balls were
found in the allotted time, but declared unplayable. What did the players do next?
A) Dropped a new ball two club-lengths from where the ball crossed
into the ravine and took a one-stroke penalty
B) Played the provisional ball and took a one-stroke penalty
C) Played the provisional ball and took a two-stroke penalty
D) Took a one-stroke penalty and returned to where they played their last shot

28 ▶

Once you've reached the hole where
your ball is resting on the lip, how long
can you wait before knocking it in?

29 ▶

What is the penalty in match play for
asking a fellow competitor what club
he hit before a particular shot?

30 ▶

How are double eagles,
eagles, birdies, bogeys,
and double bogeys
scored in the Modified
Stableford format?

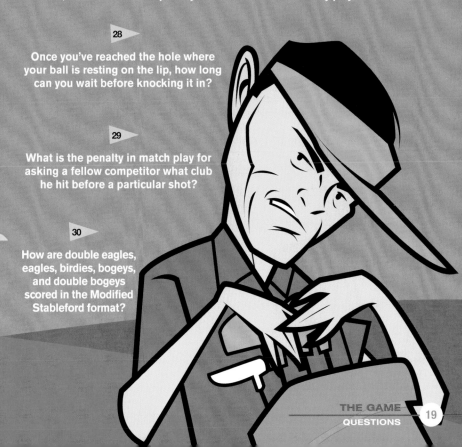

26 *One in 8,000*

27 *D) The players took a one-stroke penalty, or "stroke and distance," in which they took the penalty and returned to where they played their last shot—the tee. Once each player's first ball was found, the provisional ball was immediately abandoned.*

28 *Ten seconds. Waiting longer will incur a one-stroke penalty.*

29 *The penalty for this in match play is loss of the hole. The penalty in stroke play is two strokes.*

30 *This format, used in The INTERNATIONAL tournament, scores the following way: A double eagle is worth 8 points, an eagle is worth 5, and a birdie is worth 2. A bogey is -1 and a double bogey, -3.*

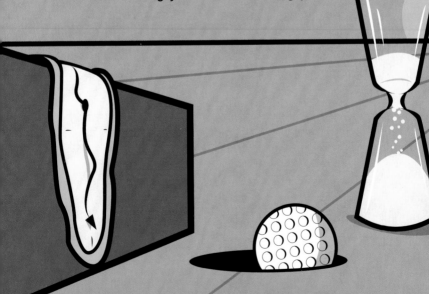

A

T. C. Chen broke me when he inadvertently
hit the ball twice during one swing of a chip shot
at the 1985 U.S. Open. What rule am I?

B

As he stood with both feet in a water hazard during
the 1991 Doral Open, Paul Azinger breached my
regulations when he moved some stones out from
under his feet before hitting his submerged ball.
What rule am I?

C

At the 2003 Royal Caribbean Golf Classic, Fuzzy
Zoeller had completed his second round and was
demonstrating proper swing technique to a local TV
personality. As he did so, he hit several shots at the
sixth hole, violating my guidelines.
What rule am I?

D

Steve Lowery's ball was resting on the 17th green at
THE PLAYERS Championship in 1997 when a seagull
picked it up and flew off, eventually dropping the
ball in the water. Fortunately, Lowery was able
to follow my stipulations and replace the stolen
ball in the spot where it had initially come to rest.
What rule am I?

E

After Andy Bean's putt lipped out at the
1983 Canadian Open, he walked up to the ball
and tapped it in with the grip end of his putter—
a clear infraction of my guidelines.
What rule am I?

WHAT RULE AM I?

WHAT RULE AM I?

A *Rule 14-4. According to this rule, Chen had to count the shot and add a one-stroke penalty. He eventually took an eight on the hole and lost the tournament to Andy North by one stroke.*

B *Rule 13-4, which states that a player cannot touch or move a loose impediment that is lying in or touching a hazard*

C *Rule 7-1b, which states that a competitor cannot practice on the course between the rounds of a stroke play competition when two or more rounds are to be played over consecutive days on that same course*

D *Rule 18-1, which states that if a ball at rest is moved by an outside agency, there is no penalty, but it must be moved back to its original location*

E *Rule 14-1, which states that the ball must be struck with the head of the club. Bean was assessed a two-stroke penalty and lost the tournament by the same margin.*

Chi Chi Rodriguez, who was inducted into the World Golf Hall of Fame in 1992, did not win the minimum of 10 PGA TOUR events to merit outright election but had won enough other victories to be inducted. How many combined PGA TOUR/Champions Tour victories must players win to qualify?
A) 15   B) 20   C) 25   D) 30

From Walter Hagen to Annika Sorenstam,
many of the game's greatest players are enshrined
in the World Golf Hall of Fame. Where is it located?
A) Ponte Vedra Beach, Florida   B) Palm Beach Gardens, Florida
C) St. Augustine, Florida   D) Far Hills, New Jersey

What former NFC passing leader attempted
to qualify for the Champions Tour in 2002?

What handicap do celebrities Alice Cooper,
Kenny G., and Donald Trump carry?
A) Scratch   B) 4   C) 10   D) 16

What percentage of
golfers maintain a
handicap?

What is the average handicap of today's golfer?
A) 14–15 B) 19–20 C) 24–25 D) 29–30

(31) **B) At least 20, assuming none of those victories is a major**

(32) **C) St. Augustine, Florida**

(33) **Steve Bartkowski of the Atlanta Falcons**

(34) **B) 4**

(35) **20 percent**

(36) **B) 19–20**

What is the average time a golf ball–
after being struck with a club–is actually
in contact with the clubface?

True or false: The average force
exerted by a clubhead while hitting
a ball is 1,000 pounds.

How much of the golf ball is
compressed upon impact?
A) One-fifth its diameter
B) One-fourth its diameter
C) One-third its diameter
D) One-half its diameter

According to the Royal and
Ancient Golf Club of St. Andrews
(R&A), what is the legal size
of a golf ball?
A) 1.62 inches   B) 1.68 inches
C) 1.88 inches   D) 2.25 inches

What is the diameter
of a golf hole?

Which of the following musicians
is not an avid golfer?
A) Robert Plant   B) Huey Lewis
C) Glenn Frey   D) Michael Bolton

What former Pittsburgh Pirates
pitcher nearly made the Champions Tour
through its annual qualifying tournament?

37 .00045 seconds, or 450 microseconds. To put that in perspective, it's significantly less than a blink of an eye.

38 False. The force is actually a much more powerful 2,000 pounds.

39 B) One-fourth its diameter

40 B) 1.68 inches, according to a 1990 ruling. This essentially marked the end of the 1.62-inch ball.

41 Exactly 4 1/4 inches

42 A) Robert Plant. The former Led Zeppelin frontman is a tennis player.

43 Rick Rhoden. A regular in the winner's circle on the Celebrity Tour, Rhoden narrowly missed qualifying in 2002 when a final-round 75 derailed his efforts. His worst previous round had been a 70—a score that, had he at least matched it, would have enabled him to finish fourth and earn his card for 2003.

By definition, why was Michelle Wie not considered a "golfer" when she competed in the Sony Open in Hawaii in 2004?

How many of the 104 World Golf Hall of Fame members are women?

According to 2000 census numbers, 51 percent of the U.S. population is female. What percent of the golfing population is female?

What is the average 18-hole score on a full-size course for men? For women?

How many annual rounds does the Tournament Players Club at Sawgrass record on average each year?
A) 35,000   B) 45,000
C) 55,000   D) 65,000

On average, how many competitive rounds did the top 10 money-making players complete on the PGA TOUR in 2003?

50

Where must a player finish on the money list to earn fully exempt status on the following year's PGA TOUR?
A) 50   B) 100   C) 125   D) 150

(44) Because Wie—who got into the tournament as a sponsor's exemption—was just 14 at the time. The official definition of a golfer is anyone age 18 or older who has played at least one regulation round of golf in the last 12 months.

(45) Twenty-eight women had been inducted as of 2004, including Marlene Stewart Streit, who became the first Canadian enshrined in 2004.

(46) 22 percent

(47) 97 and 114, respectively

(48) B) 45,000

(49) 82 rounds

(50) C) Players finishing in the top 125 earn playing privileges for the following year, while players finishing from 126–150 have only limited playing privileges.

51

Approximately how much money did Ernie Els earn in 2004 from playing in golf tournaments?

52

Which former president did Arnold Palmer play golf with?
A) Eisenhower   B) Ford   C) Nixon
D) All of the above

53

Which number is closest to what the average golfer spends each year on equipment and fees?
A) $500   B) $950   C) $1,250   D) $1,500

54

What is the average cost–including cart and green fee–at an 18-hole municipal course like New York's Bethpage? At an 18-hole daily fee course like Florida's Southern Dunes?

55

Name, in descending order, the types of courses that are most common.
A) Daily fee, municipal, private
B) Daily fee, private, municipal
C) Private, daily fee, municipal
D) Municipal, private, daily fee

56

Which of the following is not a grass commonly found on a golf course?
A) Poa annua   B) Bentgrass
C) Pythium Blight   D) Zoysia

51   *$7,725,191, which placed him second on the World Money List. $5,787,225 of that total came on the PGA TOUR.*

52   *D) All of the above*

53   *B) $950*

54   *$36 and $40, respectively*

55   *B) Daily fee, private, municipal*

56   *C) Pythium Blight is actually a destructive turf-grass disease.*

BUNKER SHOT

Texas wedge	A chip or pitch shot hit much shorter than intended
Chunky tuna	Deep, thick rough
Wormburner	A ball that hits a tree
Sky writer	A player who has been slicing all day
Beach	A ball that is hit "fat" and ends up in the water
Cake server	A player whose backswing wobbles
Mick Jagger	A golfer with little skill
Bo Derek	The cut of grass around the green that separates it from the rough
Cadillac scramble	Hitting the ball left to right rather than straight
Breaking eggs	Scoring a 10 on a hole
Strip mining	Swinging freely with the driver
Army golf	Hitting practice balls
Cabbage	A player who can't control the speed of his putts
Chili dip	A bunker
Fried egg	A ball that landed in a bunker and is half-buried
Letting the big dog eat	A ball that has misfired and ends up bouncing near parked cars
Duffer	Taking large divots every time you swing
Frog hair	A low trajectory shot that skims the ground
Hammer hands	A putt that lips out
Barkie	A putter

BUNKER SHOT

ANSWERS:

Texas wedge: A putter

Chunky tuna: A ball that is hit "fat" and ends up in the water

Wormburner: A low trajectory shot that skims the ground

Sky writer: A player whose backswing wobbles

Beach: A bunker

Cake server: A player who has been slicing all day

Mick Jagger: A putt that lips out

Bo Derek: Scoring a 10 on a hole

*Cadillac scramble: A ball that has misfired and
ends up bouncing near parked cars*

Breaking eggs: Hitting practice balls

Strip mining: Taking large divots every time you swing

Army golf: Hitting the ball left to right rather than straight

Cabbage: Deep, thick rough

Chili dip: A chip or pitch shot hit much shorter than intended

Fried egg: A ball that landed in a bunker and is half-buried

Letting the big dog eat: Swinging freely with the driver

Duffer: A golfer with little skill

*Frog hair: The cut of grass around the green
that separates it from the rough*

*Hammer hands: A player who can't control
the speed of his putts*

Barkie: A ball that hits a tree

HISTORY

From Scottish Links to Tiger's Sinks

Columbus went around the world in 1492. That isn't a lot of strokes when you consider the course.

– LEE TREVINO –

1

Many early sports, such as the 15th-century "Kolven" of Holland and "Chole" of Belgium, greatly resembled the game of golf. But what intrinsic part of the game was missing, keeping them from being considered early forms of the sport?
A) A finishing point B) Clubs C) The ball D) The hole

2

What is the earliest recorded reference to golf?

3

What was Rule No. 1 in the first written golfers' code?
A) You must play with three partners.
B) You must play the ball as it lies.
C) You must act honorably.
D) You must tee your ball within a club's length of the hole.

4

How many guidelines made up the first Rules of Golf?

5

When did golf begin in St. Andrews, Scotland?

6

When did Scotland form its Royal & Ancient (R&A) Golf Club's Rules of Golf Committee?
A) 1597 B) 1697 C) 1797 D) 1897

7

What was the original name of the USGA when it was founded in 1894?

1 *D) The hole. Both games, and many other similar ones, saw players hit balls around the landscape, but none involved dropping the ball below ground.*

2 *In 1457, King James II of Scotland banned the sport because it interfered with his subjects' archery practice.*

3 *D) You must tee your ball within a club's length of the hole.*

4 *There were 13 rules, many of which are now incorporated into the modern Rules of Golf. The original rules were written for the Edinburgh Silver Club in 1744.*

5 *The earliest surviving reference to the game is in Archbishop Hamilton's Charter in 1552, which gave St. Andrews residents the right to play golf on the linksland.*

6 *D) 1897*

7 *The Amateur Golf Association of the United States*

8

What event signaled golf's status as a global sport?
A) The creation of the Grand Slam
B) British golfer Harry Vardon's participation in the U.S. Open
C) The late 19th-century formation of the R&A and the USGA
D) Golf's designation as an Olympic sport in 1900

9

Who is considered the world's
first professional golfer?
A) "Old" Tom Morris
B) Willie Park Sr.
C) Allan Robertson
D) Andrew Strath

10

Who was the first known golfer to own
a set of custom-made clubs?

11

What types of wood were most often
used to make early golf clubs?

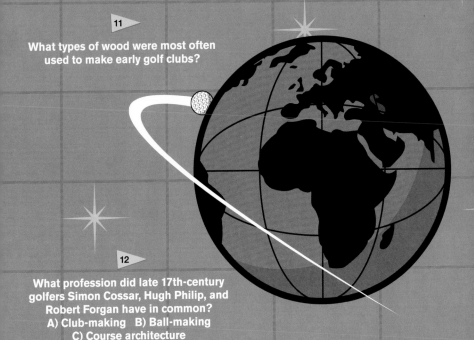

12

What profession did late 17th-century
golfers Simon Cossar, Hugh Philip, and
Robert Forgan have in common?
A) Club-making   B) Ball-making
C) Course architecture
D) Golf instruction

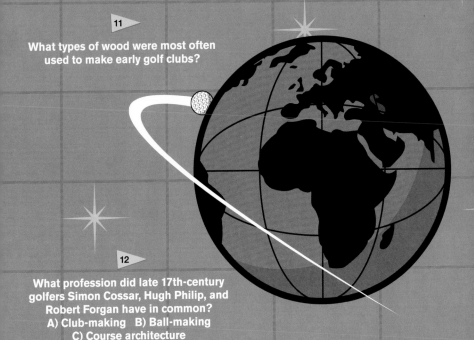

8 **D) Golf's designation as an Olympic sport in 1900. That inaugural year and the following 1904 Olympics, however, were the only times golf was included in the Games.**

9 **C) Allan Robertson. Robertson, who was the first to score below 80 on the Old Course in Scotland, was also considered the premier ball- and club-maker of the mid-19th century.**

10 **King James IV of Scotland, who in 1502 had a bow-maker build him a set**

11 **Persimmon and hickory**

12 **A) They were among the earliest known club-makers.**

13 Why did golf's long-nosed clubs, which had been around for roughly a century, become obsolete around 1850?

14 When did the Haskell ball, golf's first rubber-cored ball, debut?

15 How many extra yards was the Haskell one-piece rubber ball designed to give golfers?
A) 10 yards   B) 20 yards   C) 50 yards
D) None of the above. The ball was simply sturdier.

16 The "Featherie" ball—made from goose feathers packed inside horse- or cowhide—had a surprisingly hard shell.
In what year was it introduced?
A) 1618   B) 1718   C) 1781   D) 1881

17 Who hit the longest drive ever recorded with the Featherie ball?

18 Who won the first-known open golf championship?

19 How many players took part in the competition?
A) 11   B) 25
C) 30   D) 50

13 *The long-nosed clubs disappeared with the arrival of the "gutta percha" ball. This sturdier, more resilient ball performed more efficiently when hit with shorter club heads and irons.*

14 *At the end of the 19th century*

15 *B) 20 yards*

16 *A) 1618. The handmade balls, although expensive, were the standard for more than two centuries.*

17 *Samuel Messieux, who hit a drive of 361 yards at Elysian Fields in 1836*

18 *John Rattray won the first known open golf championship at Leith Links on April 2, 1744. Rattray later signed the original Rules of Golf.*

19 *A) 11*

20

What prize did the city of Edinburgh give
the winning golfer at Leith Links?
A) A claret jug   B) A jewel-studded belt
C) A silver club   D) A golf watch

21

How many rounds and holes did
each golfer complete during the
inaugural British Open in 1860?

22

The British Open has been part of golf
tradition since 1860. What was the cause of its
only two interruptions in play since 1900?

23

Why did gate receipts begin
to gain importance in 1892?

24

Approximately how many golf club
facilities existed in the United States by 1900?
A) 100   B) 500   C) 1,000   D) 5,000

25

What is the oldest surviving golf
club facility in the United States?

26

True or false: The Merion
Cricket Club was the
Unites States' first
18-hole golf course.

20 C) A silver club

21 Three rounds were completed on a 12-hole course, for a 36-hole total.

22 The competition was not contested from 1915 to 1919 due to World War I and from 1940 to 1945 due to World War II.

23 They were used as prize money. This first happened in Cambridge, England, after a match between Douglas Rollard and Jack White.

24 C) 1,000

25 The St. Andrews Golf Club in Yonkers, New York, which was founded in 1888

26 False. The Chicago Golf Club, which opened in 1895, holds that title. The Merion Cricket Club opened its nine-hole course in 1896, adding nine more holes in 1900.

27 What two players, aside from Francis Ouimet, were involved in the playoff of the 1913 U.S. Open?
A) Jim Barnes and Harry Vardon
B) Harry Vardon and James Braid
C) Harry Vardon and Ted Ray
D) Ted Ray and Louis Tellier

28 What did Francis Ouimet shoot in the playoff of the 1913 U.S. Open to win?
A) 70   B) 72   C) 75   D) 77

29 What was the name of Francis Ouimet's 10-year-old caddie?

30 Who founded the Walker Cup in 1922?

31 In what year did Bobby Jones win the Grand Slam?
A) 1920   B) 1925
C) 1930   D) 1935

32 In what order did Bobby Jones win the Grand Slam?
A) British Amateur, British Open, U.S. Amateur, and U.S. Open
B) British Amateur, British Open, U.S. Open, and U.S. Amateur
C) British Open, British Amateur, U.S. Open, and U.S. Amateur
D) U.S. Open, U.S. Amateur, British Amateur, and British Open

27. **C) Harry Vardon and Ted Ray**

28. **B) 72, which was five better than runner-up Harry Vardon and six better than Ted Ray**

29. **Eddie Lowery**

30. **George Herbert Walker, grandfather of George H. W. Bush, the 41st president of the United States**

31. **C) 1930**

32. **B) British Amateur, British Open, U.S. Open, and U.S. Amateur**

33

Why was Johnny Fisher's victory at the 1936 U.S. Amateur so significant?

34

John Ball is widely considered to be England's greatest amateur. How many times had he won the event when he competed in his last British Amateur in 1927?

35

Who was the first player to win both the U.S. Open and PGA Championship in the same year?

36

Gene Sarazen hit the most famous shot in golf at the 1935 Masters–a double-eagle. What club did he use?

37

Which organization first allowed the use of steel-shafted clubs, the USGA or the R&A?

38

Sarazen once lobbied–unsuccessfully– to have the golf hole increased from 4 ¹/₄ inches to what size?
A) Five inches   B) Six inches
C) Seven inches   D) Eight inches

39

What inspired Sarazen to invent the sand wedge?

33 *He was the last person to win a major using hickory-shafted clubs.*

34 *Eight times*

35 *Gene Sarazen. In 1922, the 20-year-old won the U.S. Open before going on to victory at the PGA Championship.*

36 *Sarazen used a 4-wood from 225 yards out. The shot helped him tie Craig Wood and eventually defeat him in a playoff.*

37 *The USGA was first, in 1926, followed in 1929 by the R&A.*

38 *D) Eight inches*

39 *The wings on Howard Hughes's airplane*

40

Why did Bobby Jones nickname
his putter Calamity Jane?

41

True or false: Bobby Jones
used Calamity Jane for the
remainder of his career.

42

Who owns the original
Calamity Jane putter today?
A) British Golf Museum
B) Augusta National Golf Club
C) World Golf Hall of Fame
D) United States Golf Association

43

What prompted the USGA in 1938 to limit the
number of clubs that could be carried to 14?

44

In 1949, the R&A
moved to stop slow
play. What was
the initial penalty?

45

How did the game change when
the stymie was abolished in 1952?

46

Why did Byron Nelson's
12th straight professional golf
win in 1945 go unrecognized?

HISTORY
QUESTIONS

49

40 *He didn't. The putter, already 20 years old when Jones received it in 1920, was dubbed "Calamity Jane"–named for the famous female sharpshooter of the Wild West– by its previous owner, Jim Maiden.*

41 *False. Jones began using a duplicate in 1926, which was made by Spalding and known as Calamity Jane II. With this duplicate, he won his final 10 major championships.*

42 *D) The United States Golf Association. As one of golf's most prized artifacts, Calamity Jane has an estimated value of nearly one million dollars.*

43 *Steel-shafted clubs, legalized in 1924, limited a player's shot-making ability in comparison to hickory-shafted clubs. For flexibility, golfers began carrying more and more clubs–thus forcing the USGA to place a maximum on the number a player could carry.*

44 *Disqualification. Three years later, however, the rule changed and players were disqualified only after repeated offenses.*

45 *Golfers no longer had to chip over a ball that was between their ball and the hole.*

46 *The win was not considered official because the purse was below the minimum of $5,000.*

A

I had 218 yards to go on No. 18 for a shot at an eagle putt and a 59. With my adrenaline flowing, I opted for a 5-iron instead of a 4-iron. That 5-iron helped me knock it to six feet, convert the putt for the win, and earn a spot in the history books. What history maker am I?

B

Playing in the 2000 Bell Canadian Open—with the title on the line—I found myself in a fairway bunker on No. 18, 218 yards from the hole. The final 100 yards required a carry over water. I hit a 6-iron that dropped 18 feet from the flagstick and allowed me to win. What history maker am I?

C

I holed one of the most memorable shots in Masters history when I pitched in from 140 yards out to defeat Greg Norman in 1987. What history maker am I?

D

During the final round of the 1982 U.S. Open, I used a sand wedge from 16 feet off the green in the rough and somehow salvaged a birdie, defeating Jack Nicklaus at Pebble Beach Golf Links. What history maker am I?

E

I knocked a 6-iron in from an incredible 176 yards out to defeat Scott Verplank on the first hole of a sudden-death playoff in 2004. What history maker am I?

WHAT HISTORY MAKER AM I?

A *David Duval, who at the 1999 Bob Hope Chrysler Classic became the third player on the PGA TOUR to shoot a 59*

B *Tiger Woods*

C *Larry Mize*

D *Tom Watson, who made this remarkable shot at the par-3 No. 17*

E *Craig Parry, who pulled off this feat at the Ford Championship at Doral*

47

How much money did Byron Nelson win during his
run of 11 consecutive victories in 1945?
A) $30,250   B) $50,250   C) $70,250   D) $80,250

48

In 1953 Ben Hogan won three of the four majors.
Which leg of the Grand Slam did he miss?

49

When did the PGA TOUR begin
counting the British Open as an
official TOUR victory?

50

What year is considered the formal
beginning of the PGA TOUR?

51

What event is the
oldest non-major on
the PGA TOUR?

52

The PGA TOUR is widely known
for its charitable giving. When
did the TOUR make its first
tournament donation?

53

What was the amount of the
TOUR's first donation to charity?
A) $1,000   B) $5,000
C) $10,000   D) $20,000

47 **A) $30,250, which equates to roughly $310,000 in 2003 dollars**

48 **Hogan missed the PGA Championship, because he was competing overseas in mandatory qualifying rounds for the British Open. Years later, after hearing complaints from numerous accomplished golfers who were tired of qualifying every year, Arnold Palmer helped overturn the tournament's qualifying stipulation.**

49 **Not until 1995, at which point the prize money also became official**

50 **1968, when the Tournament Players Division split from the PGA of America**

51 **The Western Open, which began in 1899**

52 **At the Palm Beach Invitational in 1938**

53 **C) $10,000**

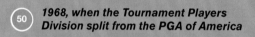

Which event offered the PGA TOUR's first $100,000 purse?
A) 1947 U.S. Open   B) 1950 Los Angeles Open
C) 1952 Bing Crosby Pro-Am   D) 1955 World Championship of Golf

When was tournament golf officially integrated?

Who was the PGA TOUR's first corporate sponsor?
A) General Motors
B) Hershey Chocolate Company
C) Spalding Sporting Goods
D) Shell Oil Company

In 1938, Babe Zaharias made history by becoming the first woman to play in a PGA TOUR event, the Los Angeles Open. Why was she invited to compete in this men's-only event?
A) She successfully "Monday qualified."
B) She petitioned the tournament.
C) She got a sponsor's exemption.
D) She won an 18-hole competition against defending champion Harry Cooper.

What was Deane Beman known for when he became the PGA TOUR's second commissioner in 1974?

Who was the PGA TOUR's first commissioner?

In 1954, after Robert Trent Jones received numerous complaints about the difficulty of his No. 4 design at Baltusrol, he played it for himself. What did he score?

54 *D) 1955 World Championship of Golf*

55 *In 1961, when the Caucasians-only clause was removed from the PGA of America constitution. Shortly thereafter, Charlie Sifford became the first African-American to play on the PGA TOUR full-time.*

56 *B) Hershey Chocolate Company, which sponsored the Hershey Open in 1933*

57 *C) She got a sponsor's exemption, which is still a practice that tournaments use today to exempt golfers with high fan interest.*

58 *Beman was the former U.S. and British Amateur champion. Incidentally, Beman grew the PGA TOUR's assets from roughly $600,000 in 1974 to $700 million when he resigned in 1994.*

59 *Joe Dey, who held the position until February of 1974*

60 *Jones proved his design was fair by making a hole-in-one.*

61

Which player employed his daughter
as the first female caddie at the Masters?
A) George Archer B) Charles Coody
C) Tommy Aaron D) Art Wall

62

Why did the Masters
reverse its front and
back nines after the first
tournament in 1934?

63

Arnold Palmer, who said goodbye to the
Masters in 2004 after 50 appearances, was
the first player to win four titles there.
In what year did he win his first?
A) 1954 B) 1956 C) 1958 D) 1960

64

Which of the following legends was not
inducted into the World Golf Hall of Fame
in Pinehurst, North Carolina, during its
1974 inaugural ceremony?
A) "Old" Tom Morris B) Francis Ouimet
C) Harry Vardon D) Walter Hagen

65

By what category were
Harvey Penick and
Karsten Solheim
inducted in to
the World Golf
Hall of Fame?

66

What club did Alan Shepard
use for his memorable
hit on the moon?
A) Sand wedge B) Driver
C) Putter D) 6-iron

67

What event, played first
in 1978, was instrumental
in helping to form the
Champions Tour?

61 **A) George Archer. In 1983, his eldest daughter, Elizabeth, caddied for him.**

62 **Bobby Jones decided the current back nine had more holes with potential drama, so he switched them.**

63 **C) 1958. Palmer would win every other year thereafter through 1964.**

64 **A) "Old" Tom Morris. He was inducted two years later.**

65 **Both men, respectively a teacher and an innovator, were enshrined via the Lifetime Achievement Category.**

66 **D) 6-iron. While its exact distance is unknown, Shepard's 1971 shot is widely considered to be the longest drive ever due to the moon's decreased gravitational pull.**

67 **The Liberty Mutual Legends of Golf. The event was played twice at Onion Creek Country Club in Texas by many of the same players—including Sam Snead, Gardner Dickinson, and Julius Boros—who helped found the Champions Tour.**

68

Who did Don January defeat by two strokes to win the 1980 Atlantic City International, the Champions Tour's first official event?
A) Miller Barber B) Gene Littler
C) Orville Moody D) Mike Souchak

69

How many tournaments did the Champions Tour have at its start?
A) 2 B) 5 C) 10 D) 12

70

What event became the fifth Champions Tour major?
A) Senior British Open B) U.S. Senior Open
C) JELD-WEN Tradition
D) Ford Senior Players Championship

71

How did Jim Ahern get into the 1999 AT&T Canada Senior Open Championship, where he earned his first Champions Tour victory?

72

When was the Champions Tour first organized?
A) 1975 B) 1980
C) 1985 D) 1990

73

What former Buick Classic winner won the United States Long Driving Championship in 1985 by hitting a 325-yard shot?

74

Which golfer owns the longest drive in major championship history?
A) Jack Nicklaus B) Tiger Woods
C) Ben Hogan D) Craig Wood

68 *D) Mike Souchak. Don January would go on to win at least one event each year through 1987, which to date is still one of the Tour's best streaks. Hale Irwin set a new mark after winning in 2004, running his streak to 10 years.*

69 *A) 2*

70 *A) Senior British Open*

71 *He "Monday qualified," which made him the seventh player to win an event after doing so.*

72 *B) 1980. At its inception, it was called the SENIOR PGA TOUR.*

73 *Dennis Paulson. After winning the long driving championship, Paulson made eight consecutive attempts at the PGA TOUR Qualifying School (Q-school) before finally getting his card in 1994.*

74 *D) Craig Wood, who blasted a 430-yard shot at No. 5 in the 1933 British Open*

What player won the 1987 South African PGA Championship and earned an invitation to the World Series of Golf, finishing second and qualifying for his PGA TOUR card?
A) Fulton Allem   B) Scott Hoch   C) Jim Thorpe   D) Bill Rogers

What eye-popping score did Jason Bohn shoot to win the Canadian Tour's 2001 Bayer Championship?
A) 57   B) 58   C) 59   D) 60

In what year did the Nationwide Tour begin?
A) 1980   B) 1985   C) 1987   D) 1990

What five players earned their PGA TOUR cards during the inaugural Nationwide Tour season?

The Nationwide Tour was originally named after what golf legend?

What was the name of the Nationwide Tour in 1996?

What company was the 2003 sponsor of the Nationwide Tour?

When did the Nationwide Tour's "Battlefield Promotion" go into effect?
A) 1990   B) 1995   C) 1997   D) 2001

(75) *A) Fulton Allem*

(76) *B) 58*

(77) *D) 1990*

(78) *Jeff Maggert, Jim McGovern, Dick Mast, Mike Springer, and Ed Humenik*

(79) *Ben Hogan. At its inception, the tournament was called the Ben Hogan Tour.*

(80) *The Nationwide Tour was called the Nike Tour from 1993 through 1999.*

(81) *Buy.com, which was announced as a replacement for Nike in late 1999*

(82) *C) In 1997. The Battlefield Promotion gives any three-time winner in a single season immediate access to the PGA TOUR.*

83

What did Doug Weaver, Mark Wiebe, Jerry Pate, and Nick Price all do on the same day of the 1989 U.S. Open?

84

What amateur pitched in on the final hole of the 1998 British Open to tie for fourth, then turned pro the next day?
A) Aaron Baddeley B) Ty Tryon
C) Justin Rose D) Adam Scott

85

What player made a hole-in-one on the 17th hole in the final round of the 1998 WAC championship to win the individual and team title?

86

What player was a surprise semifinalist at the 2001 World Golf Championships–Accenture Match Play Championship, defeating Bob Estes, Vijay Singh, Stuart Appleby, and Shigeki Maruyama along the way?

87

When was the first time Tiger Woods was featured on a Wheaties box?

(83) *They each recorded aces at the par-3 No. 6 hole.*

(84) *C) Justin Rose*

(85) *J. J. Henry of Texas Christian University*

(86) *Toru Taniguchi*

(87) *1998*

BUNKER SHOT

MATCH THE FOLLOWING GOLF CLUB OF YESTERYEAR
WITH ITS MODERN-DAY EQUIVALENT:

1-wood	Baffy
2-wood	Mid Iron
3-wood	Mashie Iron
4-wood	Cleek
1-iron	Brassie
2-iron	Mashie
3-iron	Mid Mashie
4-iron	Niblick
5-iron	Mashie Niblick
6-iron	Spoon
7-iron	Jigger
9-iron	Driver
Pitching Wedge	Spade Mashie

BUNKER SHOT

ANSWERS:

1-wood: Driver

2-wood: Brassie

3-wood: Spoon

4-wood: Baffy

1-iron: Cleek

2-iron: Mid Iron

3-iron: Mid Mashie

4-iron: Mashie Iron

5-iron: Mashie

6-iron: Spade Mashie

7-iron: Mashie Niblick

9-iron: Niblick

Pitching Wedge: Jigger

FAMOUS FIRSTS

Hitting the Sweet Spot

**Anytime a golfer hits a ball perfectly straight
with a big club it is, in my view, a fluke.**

– JACK NICKLAUS –

1

What is the first known reference to golf in the United States?

2

Who was the first known female golfer?

3

Who won the men's and women's individual gold medals for golf in the 1900 Olympics, the first time the sport was featured in the Games?

4

Where was the term "birdie" first coined?

5

Who had the first recorded hole-in-one?
A) "Old" Tom Morris   B) "Young" Tom Morris
C) Willie Park   D) Allan Robertson

6

Who was the first player to break 80 at The Old Course at St. Andrews?

7

Why was Willie Anderson's win at the 1902 Western Open so significant?

8

Who was the first American to win the British Amateur?

1 *In 1659, golf was banned from the streets in Albany, New York.*

2 *Mary, Queen of Scots, who raised more than a few eyebrows when she was seen playing golf shortly after her husband's death in 1567*

3 *Charles Sands and Margaret Abbott of the United States*

4 *At the Atlantic City Country Club in New Jersey in 1898. There, a member described a well-played shot as a "bird of a shot."*

5 *B) "Young" Tom Morris, who aced the 145-yard eighth hole at Prestwick at the 1868 British Open*

6 *Allan Robertson, who shot a 79 in 1858*

7 *Anderson, who scored 299, was the first to shoot under 300 in a 72-hole event in the United States.*

8 *Walter J. Travis, in 1904*

9

Who was the first American captain of the Royal and Ancient Golf Club of St. Andrews?

10

Who was the first player to win both the U.S. Open and the U.S. Amateur?
A) Chick Evans   B) Tiger Woods
C) Jack Nicklaus   D) Francis Ouimet

11

True or false: Bobby Jones played in his first U.S. Amateur at the age of 14.

12

Who was the first player to win a major using the Haskell wound rubber ball?

13

What year did Bobby Jones win his first major championship?

14

When was the first dimpled golf ball invented?

15

In what year did groove-faced irons first make their appearance?
A) 1898   B) 1902
C) 1905   D) 1909

9   *Francis Ouimet received that honor in 1951.*

10 *D) Francis Ouimet. He won the U.S. Open in 1913 and the U.S. Amateur the following year.*

11 *True. The 14-year-old played in 1916.*

12 *Walter J. Travis, who did so at the 1901 U.S. Amateur*

13 *In 1923 at the U.S. Open, when he defeated Bobby Cruickshank in a playoff*

14 *William Taylor invented the sport's first dimpled ball in 1905.*

15 *B) 1902*

16 ▶
What was introduced first,
metalwood or the graphite shaft?

17 ▶
Why was Billy Burke's win at the
1931 U.S. Open such a milestone?

18 ▶
Who was the first golfer
to endorse a product?

19 ▶
Who was the first player to begin a
golf company using his name?

20 ▶
What was the first golf book published in America?
A) *Golf in America: A Practical Manual* by James Lee
B) *The Complete Golfer* by Harry Vardon
C) *The Golf Courses of the British Isles* by Bernard Darwin
D) None of the above

21 ▶
Why was Jim Barnes's book
Picture Analysis of Golf Strokes
so groundbreaking?

16 *The graphite shaft made its debut in 1973. Metalwood was introduced by TaylorMade six years later.*

17 *Burke, who defeated George Von Elm in a playoff, was the first player to win a major with steel-shafted clubs.*

18 *Harry Vardon, who used the "Vardon Flyer" ball during his exhibition tour of America in 1900*

19 *Walter Hagen. He began the Walter Hagen Golf Company in 1922.*

20 *A)* Golf in America: A Practical Manual, *written by James Lee in 1895*

21 *Published in 1919, it was the first golf book to use high-speed sequence photography.*

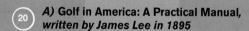

22

When was *Golf*, the United States'
first golfing magazine, published?

 23

When was golf first telecast?

 24

Which was the first nationally televised golf tournament?
A) The 1953 World Championship
B) The 1955 Tam O'Shanter Invitational
C) The 1956 U.S. Open
D) The 1957 Western Open

 25

Which clubhouse was built first?
A) Golf House at Leith
B) South Carolina Golf Club
C) Royal Montreal Golf Club
D) Royal Aberdeen Golf Club

 26

The first practice range in the
United States opened in
1920. What city was it in?

 27

Where was the first complete
fairway irrigation system installed?

28

In what order did the following golf courses open?
A) Pebble Beach Golf Links,
Pinehurst No. 2, Augusta National
B) Pebble Beach Golf Links, Augusta
National, Pinehurst No. 2
C) Pinehurst No. 2, Augusta
National, Pebble Beach Golf Links
D) Pinehurst No. 2, Pebble Beach
Golf Links, Augusta National

22 *1897*

23 *The 1947 U.S. Open was broadcast locally in St. Louis. The event was played at the St. Louis Country Club.*

24 *A) The 1953 World Championship, in which Lew Worsham holed out for an eagle from 135 yards to win*

25 *A) The Golf House at Leith in Edinburgh was built first, in 1768, followed by the Royal Aberdeen Golf Club in 1780. The South Carolina Golf Club of Charleston, the first club in the United States, dates to 1786. The Royal Montreal Golf Club, Canada's first club, was built nearly a century later, in 1873.*

26 *Pinehurst, North Carolina*

27 *At Brook Hollow Golf Club in Dallas, in 1925*

28 *D) Pinehurst No. 2 (1901), Pebble Beach Golf Links (1919), and Augusta National (1933)*

29

Which of the following PGA TOUR
events was played first?
A) HP Classic of New Orleans
B) Shell Houston Open
C) AT&T Pebble Beach National Pro-Am
D) Valero Texas Open

30

When Horton Smith won the tournament
now known as The Masters for the first time
in 1934, what was it called?

31

What was the first name of
the AT&T Pebble Beach
National Pro-Am?

32

Which of the following tournaments is correctly
identified with its original name?
A) Palm Springs Golf Classic: Nissan Open
B) Tournament of Champions: The Mercedes Championship
C) Jackie Gleason's Inverrary Classic: Bay Hill Invitational
D) Home of the Sun Invitational: Chrysler Classic of Tucson

33

When did the PGA
Championship first switch
from a match-play event to
a stroke-play event?

34

The first year an admission
fee was charged for the U.S. Open
was 1922. How much was it?

35

When did the USGA first
have sectional qualifying
for the U.S. Open?
A) 1921 B) 1924
C) 1927 D) 1930

29 *D) The Valero Texas Open debuted before the others, in 1922.*

30 *Augusta National Invitational*

31 *Bing Crosby Professional-Amateur*

32 *B) The Mercedes Championship was originally known as the Tournament of Champions, from 1953 to 1974.*

33 *In 1958, when Dow Finsterwald defeated Billy Casper by two strokes*

34 *The fee was $1. Today the U.S. Open is so popular that fans have to apply for tickets. The tournament then conducts a random drawing and notifies the winners by mail that they are eligible to purchase tickets.*

35 *B) 1924*

36

The 1976 U.S. Open was the first to be played in the deep South. Where was it contested?

37

What was the first state to host two Ryder Cups?

38

When was the first time the United States won the Ryder Cup on British soil?

39

What year did Great Britain win its first Ryder Cup?

40

What was the score of the first Presidents Cup?

41

How many holes were played in the first PGA TOUR National Qualifying Tournament in 1965?
A) 72   B) 90   C) 108   D) 144

42

Who was the first African-American to play on the PGA TOUR?
A) Charlie Sifford
B) Pete Brown
C) Bill Spiller
D) Lee Elder

36 *Atlanta Athletic Club in Georgia*

37 *California. The 1955 matches were played at Thunderbird Ranch and Country Club in Palm Springs, and the 1959 matches were played at Eldorado Country Club in Palm Desert.*

38 *1937. The score was 8 to 4.*

39 *In 1929, at the second Ryder Cup contest*

40 *The United States won the 1994 tournament 20 to 12.*

41 *D) 144*

42 *C) Bill Spiller, who participated in the 1948 Los Angeles Open*

A ▶

I established myself as one of the game's best putters, ranking first on the PGA TOUR in putting average in 1996, 1999, and 2000. What record breaker am I?

B ▶

As one of the PGA TOUR's greatest players, I was ranked first on the Official World Golf Ranking 11 different times for a total of 331 weeks, and was inducted into the World Golf Hall of Fame in 2001. What record breaker am I?

C ▶

I am not one of the longest hitters on the PGA TOUR, but I am certainly one of the most accurate. I was first in driving accuracy in 1995, 1996, 1999, 2000, 2002, and 2003. What record breaker am I?

D ▶

From 1980 to 2003, only two players have led the PGA TOUR in sand saves for more than one year. I am the only one to hold this record for three years, ranking first in 1986, 1987, and 1990. What record breaker am I?

WHAT RECORD BREAKER AM I?

A *Brad Faxon*

B *Greg Norman*

C *Fred Funk*

D *Paul Azinger*

43

Who was the first African-American
to win on the PGA TOUR?

44

Which golfer was the first to successfully
defend his title at the Bob Hope Chrysler Classic?
A) Arnold Palmer   B) Billy Casper
C) Johnny Miller   D) Tom Kite

45

Who was the first player to win all the
modern-day professional majors twice?

46

What United States president did Arnold Palmer meet
shortly after winning his first Masters in 1958?

47

Who was the first player to break
60 on the PGA TOUR?

48

Who was the first to break 270 at THE PLAYERS
Championship on the Tournament Players Club at Sawgrass?
A) Jack Nicklaus   B) Nick Price
C) Greg Norman   D) Fred Couples

43 *Pete Brown, who won the 1964 Waco Turner Open*

44 *C) Johnny Miller, in 1976. As of 2004, he was the only person to do so.*

45 *Jack Nicklaus achieved this record by 1971. With the exception of the British Open, he has won every major at least four times.*

46 *Dwight D. Eisenhower. The president, who initially did not recognize Arnold Palmer as being the legendary golfer, wrote him a letter a short time later, apologizing for not making the connection. That began a lifelong friendship between the two men.*

47 *Al Geiberger, in 1977*

48 *C) Greg Norman, who shot a 264 in 1994*

49

Who was the first player to win his first
two starts on the Champions Tour?
A) Hale Irwin B) Gil Morgan
C) Bruce Fleisher D) Jack Nicklaus

50

Who was the first player
age 60 or older to win
on the Champions Tour?

51

Who won the Nationwide
Tour's first event?

52

What player was the first to earn a
"Battlefield Promotion" to the PGA TOUR?

53

Who recorded the first 59 in the
history of the Nationwide Tour?
A) Doug Dunakey B) Notah Begay III
C) David Duval D) David Toms

54

Who was the first player to win
back-to-back Vardon Trophies?
A) Ben Hogan B) Arnold Palmer
C) Billy Casper D) Sam Snead

55

Who won the
first Vardon
Trophy in 1937?

49 *C) Bruce Fleisher. In 1999, he won the Royal Caribbean Golf Classic and the American Express Invitational on his way to receiving Rookie of the Year honors.*

50 *Roberto De Vicenzo, who won the Merrill Lynch/Golf Digest Commemorative in 1984 at age 61*

51 *Mike Springer won the Bakersfield Open, which began in California on February 2, 1990.*

52 *Chris Smith*

53 *B) Notah Begay III achieved this historic milestone at the 1998 Dominion Open. Doug Dunakey followed three weeks later at the Miami Valley Open.*

54 *A) Ben Hogan, who did so in 1940 and 1941*

55 *Harry Cooper, who won the first and only one of his career. The trophy is awarded each year by the PGA of America to the PGA TOUR player who posts the season's best scoring average. It changed to an adjusted scoring average in 1988.*

56

Who won the first Payne Stewart Award in 2000?
A) Byron Nelson   B) Jack Nicklaus
C) Arnold Palmer   D) All of the above

57

True or false: Curtis Strange was the first player to win
the Arnold Palmer Award consecutively, in 1985 and 1986.

58

Who was the first player to win consecutive
Jack Nicklaus Trophies as Player of the Year?
A) Nick Price   B) Fred Couples
C) Greg Norman   D) Tiger Woods

59

What is the prize for finishing first
in adjusted scoring average?

60

What does the golfer who finishes
first at the Masters receive
as a lifetime award?
A) Membership at Augusta National
B) Entrance into the tournament
C) Admittance to the PGA TOUR
D) All of the above

61

Who received
the PGA TOUR's first
Lifetime Achievement
Award in 1996?

56 *D) All of the above. The three legends shared the award, which honors players who respect the traditions of the game and continue its heritage of charity.*

57 *False. Strange was the first to win the award consecutively, but he did it in 1987 and 1988.*

58 *B) Fred Couples, in 1991 and 1992*

59 *The Byron Nelson Award*

60 *B) Entrance into the tournament*

61 *Gene Sarazen*

What is the prize for finishing first on
the PGA TOUR official money list?

Who was the first player to surpass
$100,000 in earnings in a single season?

Who was the first player to surpass
$500,000 in earnings in a single season?

Which player was the first to reach $1 million
in earnings during a single Skins Game?
A) Greg Norman   B) Fred Couples
C) Tom Watson   D) Mark O'Meara

John Daly led the PGA TOUR in
driving distance from 1995 to 2002.
During that time span, when did his
average first exceed 300 yards?
A) 1995   B) 1997   C) 1999   D) 2001

The PGA TOUR had a record
number of first-time winners in
2002. How many were there?
A) 10   B) 13   C) 16   D) 18

62 *The Arnold Palmer Award*

63 *Arnold Palmer, who took home $128,230 in 1963*

64 *Tom Watson, who pocketed $530,808.33 in 1980*

65 *A) Greg Norman, who won a cool million in 2001*

66 *B) 1997, when he averaged 302 yards*

67 *D) 18*

BUNKER SHOT

Jack Nicklaus	1971 Sea Pines Heritage Classic
Arnold Palmer	1993 Buick Classic
Tiger Woods	1996 Buick Open
Ernie Els	1999 Air Canada Championship
Phil Mickelson	1983 Kemper Open
Vijay Singh	2001 MasterCard Colonial
Jim Furyk	1955 Canadian Open
Davis Love III	1974 Western Open
Mike Weir	1991 Northern Telecom Open
Fred Couples	1978 Greater Greensboro Open
Justin Leonard	1987 MCI Heritage Golf Classic
John Daly	1962 U.S. Open
Greg Norman	1973 San Antonio Texas Open
Hale Irwin	1994 U.S. Open
Sergio Garcia	1995 Las Vegas Invitational
Nick Faldo	1976 IVB-Bicentennial Golf Classic
Ben Crenshaw	1984 Kemper Open
Tom Watson	1991 PGA Championship
Tom Kite	1996 Las Vegas Invitational
Seve Ballesteros	1984 Sea Pines Heritage

BUNKER SHOT

ANSWERS:

Jack Nicklaus: 1962 U.S. Open

Arnold Palmer: 1955 Canadian Open

Tiger Woods: 1996 Las Vegas Invitational

Ernie Els: 1994 U.S. Open

Phil Mickelson: 1991 Northern Telecom Open

Vijay Singh: 1993 Buick Classic

Jim Furyk: 1995 Las Vegas Invitational

Davis Love III: 1987 MCI Heritage Golf Classic

Mike Weir: 1999 Air Canada Championship

Fred Couples: 1983 Kemper Open

Justin Leonard: 1996 Buick Open

John Daly: 1991 PGA Championship

Greg Norman: 1984 Kemper Open

Hale Irwin: 1971 Sea Pines Heritage Classic

Sergio Garcia: 2001 MasterCard Colonial

Nick Faldo: 1984 Sea Pines Heritage

Ben Crenshaw: 1973 San Antonio Texas Open

Tom Watson: 1974 Western Open

Tom Kite: 1976 IVB-Bicentennial Golf Classic

Seve Ballesteros: 1978 Greater Greensboro Open

THE PLAYERS
They Hit It Like Hogan

I'm only afraid of three things:
lightning, a sidehill putt, and Ben Hogan.

– SAM SNEAD –

1

Where was Vijay Singh born?
A) The United States B) Fiji
    C) India D) Malaysia

 2

What was Italian American Gene
    Sarazen's birth name?

 3

What player fled Czechoslovakia as a nine-year-old
refugee and traveled with his father to Yugoslavia,
Italy, and Switzerland before settling in Germany
and finally returning to Prague in 1997?
A) Bernhard Langer B) Alex Cejka
    C) Thomas Bjorn D) Peter Lonard

 4

True or false: Tiger Woods was nicknamed after
his dad, a soldier who fought in Vietnam.

 5

What father-son tandem won their
respective PGA TOUR and Champions Tour
events on the same day in 1999?

 6

Which brothers have both won on the PGA TOUR?
A) Mike and Dave Hill B) David and Kevin Sutherland
    C) Curt and Tom Byrum D) Both A and C

 7

What two-time
U.S. Open champ
has a twin brother
named Allen?

1. *B) Fiji*

2. *Eugenio Saraceni. He changed his name at age 16 to Sarazen because "it sounded like a golfer."*

3. *B) Alex Cejka, who still considers himself German*

4. *False. Born Eldrick Woods, the golf champ was actually given the name "Tiger" after his father's army friend who went by the same nickname.*

5. *Bob and David Duval. David won THE PLAYERS Championship the same day his father won the Emerald Coast Classic: March 28, 1999.*

6. *D) Both A and C. The Hill brothers and the Byrum brothers have both won PGA TOUR events. Dave Hill has won 13 times, while Mike has won three times. Curt and Tom Byrum have each won once.*

7. *Curtis Strange*

8

Why did Jesper Parnevik name his son Phoenix?

9

Why is Jesper Parnevik's father famous in Sweden?
A) He's one of the country's top comedians.
B) He anchors the national evening news.
C) He's an award-winning character actor.
D) He hosts a syndicated talk radio show.

10

Which player, at age 60, adopted twin infant sons in 1999?

11

True or false: J. C. Snead is the nephew of golf legend Sam Snead.

12

How is Don Haskins associated with the PGA TOUR?

13

Name the PGA TOUR player whose father was a major league baseball pitcher and whose uncle is a member of the National Baseball Hall of Fame.

14

What player's father was an outfielder for the New York Yankees, Chicago White Sox, St. Louis Browns, and Kansas City A's?

8 *Because he won his first PGA TOUR title at the 1998 Phoenix Open.*

9 *A) He's one of the country's top comedians.*

10 *Jim Dent*

11 *True*

12 *He is Steve Haskins's dad. The elder Haskins, the legendary former University of Texas-El Paso basketball coach, won more than 700 games.*

13 *Chris Perry. His father, Jim, pitched for four teams and his uncle is baseball great Gaylord Perry.*

14 *Jay Delsing's father, Jim*

15

After what legendary baseball player did
Robert "Spike" McRoy get his nickname?
A) Ty Cobb   B) Lou Brock
C) Honus Wagner   D) Lou Gehrig

16

What is Fuzzy Zoeller's full name?

17

What is Duffy Waldorf's
real first name?
A) James   B) Joseph
C) John   D) Jack

18

What do K. J. Choi's initials stand for?

19

What former back-to-back U.S. Amateur
winner named his dog "Replace All Divots"?

20

What player got married
on the 18th green at the
Tournament Players Club
at Las Colinas prior to the
start of the 1994 EDS Byron
Nelson Championship?

21

Who first met his wife
at the 1985 Texas Open and
then married her at the
event one year later?

ANSWERS

15 A) McRoy got his nickname from Ty Cobb, an aggressive base runner who often left high spike marks on second basemen.

16 Frank Urban Zoeller

17 A) James

18 Kyoung-Ju

19 Jay Sigel

20 Billy Mayfair

21 David Ogrin

22

Who is Jay Haas's uncle?

23

True or false:
Dennis and Carl Paulson
are cousins.

24

What is the relationship
between Padraig Harrington and
NFL quarterback Joey Harrington?
A) Brothers B) Brothers-in-law
C) Uncle and nephew D) Cousins

25

Whose father, Johan, is
commissioner of the
Sunshine Tour?
A) Trevor Immelman
B) Rory Sabbatini
C) Tim Clark
D) Retief Goosen

26

What three-time PGA TOUR winner had a
father, Charlie, who played tackle for the
Oakland Raiders and a brother, Chuck, who
played for the St. Louis Cardinals?

27

What Olympic sport did Robert Garrigus's father coach?
A) Basketball B) Diving C) Pole vaulting D) Shooting

28

Which player's
father-in-law, Ralph
Kiner, is in the Baseball
Hall of Fame?
A) Robin Freeman
B) Kelly Gibson
C) Hank Kuehne
D) Todd Fischer

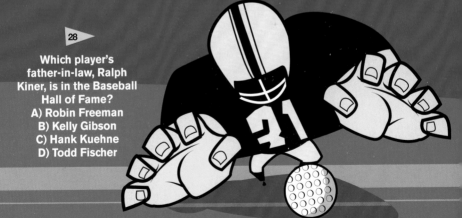

22 *Bob Goalby, who won the 1968 Masters*

23 *False. The two are not related.*

24 *D) Cousins*

25 *A) Trevor Immelman*

26 *Billy Ray Brown*

27 *D) Shooting*

28 *A) Robin Freeman*

29 What LPGA superstar is married to former baseball player Ray Knight?

30 What family did Lee Westwood marry into in 1999?

31 What two players married sisters Soozi and Rose?

32 Which PGA TOUR player is married to Jesper Parnevik's sister?
A) Per-Ulrik Johansson
B) Mathias Gronberg
C) Daniel Chopra
D) Gabriel Hjertstedt

33 Which golfing brother is older, Bobby or Lanny Wadkins?

34 Chi Chi Rodriguez grew up very poor and was forced to craft his own golf clubs and balls. What materials did he use?

29 *Nancy Lopez. They married in 1982.*

30 *The Coltart family. Westwood married Laurae Coltart, sister of golfer Andrew Coltart.*

31 *Jerry Pate and Bruce Lietzke*

32 *A) Per-Ulrik Johansson is married to Jesper's sister Jill.*

33 *Lanny is older by roughly 18 months.*

34 *He made clubs from guava branches and balls from hammering tin cans into round shapes.*

Why did Charles Coody begin playing golf?

Georgian Franklin Langham began going to the Masters at age eight and worked at the tournament while he was in high school. What was his job?
A) He sold concessions.
B) He worked as a media officer.
C) He caddied.
D) He worked the 16th-hole leader board.

Which of the following is true about Fredrik Jacobson?
A) As a 10-year-old, he was a promising hockey player.
B) During his middle teen years he was a top-30 ranked Swedish table tennis player.
C) He became a scratch golfer at age 15.
D) All of the above

What ailment caused a young Andy North to take a break from basketball and football and begin playing golf?

What eventual LPGA founder quarterbacked a neighborhood football team in Minneapolis known as the "50th Street Tigers," a team that also featured future legendary coach Bud Wilkinson at tackle?
A) Babe Zaharias   B) Patty Berg
C) Louise Suggs   D) Marilynn Smith

35 *He had polio as a child and was not allowed to play contact sports, so he took up golf.*

36 *D) He worked the 16th-hole leader board.*

37 *D) All of the above*

38 *He had a disintegrating knee bone as a teenager.*

39 *B) Patty Berg, who has a signed football on permanent display in her locker at the World Golf Hall of Fame*

40

Identify the following teammates with their correct alma mater:
A) Brigham Young University: Bob Friend, Emlyn Aubrey, and David Toms
B) University of Hawaii: Dean Wilson and Mike Weir
C) University of Nevada: Chad Campbell, Ed Fryatt, and Chris Riley
D) Northern Arizona University: Morris Hatalsky, Tom Purtzer, and Howard Twitty

41

Which of the following combination of players
were not college teammates?
A) Marco Dawson, Lee Janzen, and Cliff Kresge
B) Chris DiMarco, Dudley Hart, and Pat Bates
C) Blaine McCallister and Fred Couples
D) Rick Fehr, Richard Zokol, and Keith Clearwater

42

Who won the 1992 World Amateur Championships,
then went on to attend the University of Arizona,
winning seven collegiate titles there?
A) Lorena Ochoa   B) Natalie Gulbis
C) Tina Tombs   D) Annika Sorenstam

43

What two members of the 1986 NCAA
Championship team at Wake Forest
went on to win PGA TOUR events?

44

Who was a member of the 18-and-under
French field hockey team and was ranked
14th nationally as a tennis player?

45

True or false: Boo Weekley and
Heath Slocum played on the same
high school golf team in Florida.

40 *C) Campbell, Fryatt, and Riley were teammates at the University of Nevada–Las Vegas. Fryatt graduated in 1994, while Campbell and Riley graduated two years later.*

41 *A) Marco Dawson and Lee Janzen were teammates at Florida Southern College, but Cliff Kresge played a few hours north at the University of Central Florida.*

42 *D) Annika Sorenstam, who was also an NCAA All-American from 1991 to 1992*

43 *Billy Andrade and Len Mattiace*

44 *Thomas Levet*

45 *True. They played in Milton, Florida, a small town in the state's panhandle.*

46

What do Jack Nicklaus, Ted Tryba, and Joey Sindelar have in common?

47

What former college teammate did Corey Pavin caddy for during the 2003 PGA TOUR National Qualifying Tournament?
A) Jay Delsing   B) Duffy Waldorf
C) Tom Pernice Jr.   D) Steve Pate

48

What Champions Tour player batted .421 at Bucknell–one of the highest totals in school history–in 1962 as a baseball player?
A) J. C. Snead   B) Jim Albus
C) Tom Wargo   D) Kermit Zarley

49

What PGA TOUR and Champions Tour superstar was named to the University of Colorado's All-Century Football Team?

50

What former Morgan State running back has enjoyed career-defining success since joining the Champions Tour in 1999?

51

What prompted golfer Jason Bohn, then a student at the University of Alabama, to give up his amateur status in 1992?

46 *They all attended Ohio State.*

47 *A) Jay Delsing*

48 *B) Jim Albus*

49 *Hale Irwin, who was a quarterback and a two-time All-Big Eight selection as a defensive back*

50 *Jim Thorpe*

51 *He made an ace during a hole-in-one shootout that was worth $1 million—but only a professional could accept the prize.*

52 ▶

How many times did Nationwide Tour grad Justin Bolli have to walk on to his college team at the University of Georgia?
A) None. He was recruited out of high school.
B) Once as a sophomore
C) Three times   D) Four times

53 ▶

What Nationwide Tour player was a substitute teacher at the time of his victory at the 1992 Yuma Open?

54 ▶

Which player took time off after the 1991 Nationwide Tour season, obtained a license to sell insurance, and took a job stacking boxes and filling orders in the golf retail business before setting the 90-hole scoring record on the PGA TOUR?
A) Joe Durant   B) Paul Stankowski
C) John Cook   D) Mark Calcavecchia

55 ▶

What member of the World Golf Hall of Fame has a stud farm?

56 ▶

Which player quit golf in 1995 to sell cell phones and car stereos in Seattle, and then returned to the game, earning his PGA TOUR card via Q-school in 1998?

57 ▶

What winner of the Mexican Open was previously a professional boxer?

52 *C) Three times*

53 *Paul Goydos*

54 *A) Joe Durant. He had a 324 total (36-under-par) at the 2001 Bob Hope Chrysler Classic.*

55 *Gary Player. He has a 10,000-acre farm near Colesberg in South Africa.*

56 *Rich Beem, who went on to win the PGA Championship in 2000*

57 *Esteban Toledo*

58

What golfer is a former provincial and national speed skating champ in Canada?
A) Mike Weir B) Richard Zokol
C) Ian Leggatt D) Both B and C

59

What minor league hockey team did John Harris play for in 1975?

60

What sports did Babe Zaharias medal in during the 1932 Olympics?

61

Which Swedish player has had seven broken ribs and a broken hand and foot, and once competed in his country's skateboarding championship?
A) Anders Forsbrand B) Daniel Chopra
C) Fredrik Jacobson D) Richard S. Johnson

62

What was Cary Middlecoff's job before he became a professional golfer?
A) Veterinarian B) Mechanic
C) Encyclopedia salesman
D) Dentist

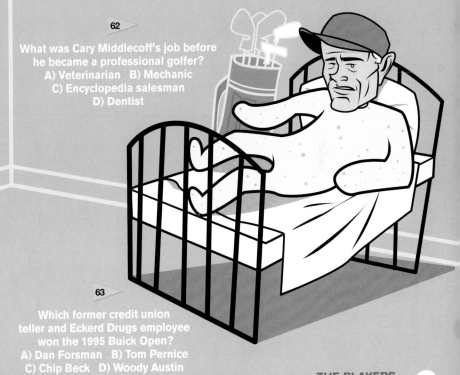

63

Which former credit union teller and Eckerd Drugs employee won the 1995 Buick Open?
A) Dan Forsman B) Tom Pernice
C) Chip Beck D) Woody Austin

58 **C) Ian Leggatt**

59 **The New England Whalers**

60 *She won the gold in the javelin throw and 80-meter hurdles. She also was awarded a half-gold/half-silver after the Games because of her controversial performance in the high jump: her use of the "Western Roll" technique to clear the high jump bar. This newer method involved clearing the bar head first rather than feet first.*

61 **D) Richard S. Johnson**

62 **D) Dentist**

63 **D) Woody Austin**

64

What job did Mark Johnson have for 18 years before beginning his professional golf career?
A) Stockbroker   B) Firefighter
C) Beer truck driver
D) Owner of a pizza chain restaurant

65

"Old" Tom Morris, the most revered figure in Scottish golf history, was a greenskeeper at what historic course?
A) Prestwick   B) St. Andrews
C) Royal County Down   D) Both A and B

66

Legendary golf teacher Harvey Penick's pupils included Ben Crenshaw, Kathy Whitworth, and Mickey Wright. What was Penick's other full-time job?

67

Where did Fred Funk coach golf for most of the 1980s?

68

What LPGA winner graduated cum laude from Yale University, was the school's women's golf coach from 1997 to 2000, and still serves as a teacher and recruiter?

69

What former PGA TOUR and USGA employee was a winner on the Champions Tour in 2003?

64 *C) He drove a beer truck.*

65 *D) Both A and B. Morris designed Royal County Down.*

66 *Head golf coach at the University of Texas*

67 *The University of Maryland*

68 *Heather Daly-Donofrio. She also attended Oxford University in England.*

69 *David Eger, who won the MasterCard Classic*

70

What three-time Champions Tour winner
was the mayor of Toco, Texas?

71

Who ran for the Australian Parliament in
1982 and lost by a narrow margin?
A) Greg Norman   B) Peter Thomson
C) Stuart Appleby   D) Robert Allenby

72

Which PGA TOUR star began working
as an analyst on USA Network's
PGA TOUR Sunday in 2003?

73

Which of the following is true about Greg Norman?
A) He's in the men's sportswear business.
B) He's in the turf grass business.
C) He's in the wine business.
D) All of the above

74

Which player wrote about his first year on
the PGA TOUR in the book *Rookie on Tour*?
A) Carl Paulson   B) Dennis Paulson
C) Brenden Pappas   D) Deane Pappas

MAYOR

70 *Rocky Thompson. He resigned the post on September 10, 1998, after being in office for 15 years.*

71 *B) Peter Thomson*

72 *John Cook*

73 *D) All of the above*

74 *A) Carl Paulson*

75

What player is author of *Golf for Dummies* and *Just a Range Ball in a Box Full of Titleists*?

76

What former PGA TOUR champion and longtime Bible student has published books including *Palestine Is Coming* and *The Gospels Interwoven*?

77

Which of Ben Crenshaw's books was a *New York Times* bestseller?

78

Where does Kenny Perry donate five percent of his earnings?
A) University of Kentucky
B) Western Kentucky University
C) David Lipscomb University
D) Bethel College

79

Who had a large hand in building Kansas State University's new golf course?

80

What is Gil Morgan a doctor of?

75 *Gary McCord*

76 *Kermit Zarley*

77 **A Feel for the Game**

78 *C) Perry donates part of his earnings to his wife's alma mater, David Lipscomb University, a Christian college in Nashville, Tennessee.*

79 *Jim Colbert, who assisted with the aptly named Colbert Hills Golf Club*

80 *Optometry. He keeps his license current though he has never practiced.*

A

I graduated with a mechanical engineering degree from Georgia Tech, held an English literature degree from Harvard, and attended law school. I had an unprecedented season in 1930, winning all four majors of the day. The clubhouse flag at The Old Course at St. Andrews was lowered to half-mast when I died on December 18, 1971. What player am I?

B

I'm a former Australian Rules football player who has won on the Nationwide Tour and PGA TOUR as well as in Australia. Each year in New South Wales, a memorial trophy honoring my late wife is given to the state's top female junior golfer. What player am I?

C

My golf roots run deep. My grandfather won the U.S. Open, British Open, and PGA Championship, and is now in the World Golf Hall of Fame. I've won several times on the PGA TOUR myself, including the 2003 Valero Texas Open, where I set the PGA TOUR's 72-hole scoring record. What player am I?

D

As a high school senior, I struggled on the golf course because I didn't practice, instead working in my father's marina pumping gas and painting boats. My game improved markedly when I enrolled in Brevard Junior College. Since then I've won on the PGA TOUR more than 10 times, including a major championship. What player am I?

E

The 2002 movie *Windtalkers* featured the 375 Native Americans who helped the U.S. government with intelligence during World War II. My grandfather was among those men, serving as a radioman on the front line. I won twice on the PGA TOUR in 1999–becoming the first Native American to win since 1974–and was nominated for Rookie of the Year. What player am I?

WHAT PLAYER AM I?

WHAT PLAYER AM I?

(A) *Bobby Jones*

(B) *Stuart Appleby*

(C) *Tommy Armour III*

(D) *Paul Azinger*

(E) *Notah Begay III*

81

What two-time winner of
THE PLAYERS Championship is
a talented caricature artist?

82

What player's website is
www.gripitandripit.com?

83

What website allows Aaron
Baddeley fans to join his club?

84

What was the title of Davis
Love III's book, which paid tribute
to his dad's teachings?

85

What player donated a
trophy in 1952 in the name
of Glenna Collett Vare,
which is given out annually
to the LPGA Tour's scoring
average leader?
A) Betty Jameson
B) Bettye Danoff
C) Helen Hicks
D) Opal Hill

81 *Steve Elkington*

82 *John Daly*

83 *www.badds.com*

84 Every Shot I Take

85 *A) Betty Jameson, the first woman to break 300 in a 72-hole tournament, donated the trophy at the 1947 U.S. Women's Open.*

86

What player donated $100,000
to the Arnold Palmer Children's
Hospital in Orlando after winning
the 1989 Las Vegas Invitational?

 87

Which player places on his golf bag the
image of a missing child from each tournament city
he plays in to raise awareness and to encourage
the return of the child to his or her family?
A) Dean Wilson   B) Kirk Triplett
C) Briny Baird   D) Robert Game

 88

What player features pictures of children in
need of adoption on his golf bag each week?

 89

What two PGA TOUR players
cohost the CVS Charity Classic
each year to benefit children
in their New England
home states?

 90

What American played
in the 2004 British Open with
a golf bag featuring patches
from various military divisions
to support their efforts in the
fight against terrorism?

86 *Scott Hoch*

87 *C) Briny Baird*

88 *Kirk Triplett*

89 *Brad Faxon and Billy Andrade*

90 *Frank Lickliter, who also made a trip to Guantanamo Bay to bring golf supplies to the military personnel stationed there*

DENT, JIM

91

Why does Jim Dent carry $50 in his wallet at all times?

92

Which Nationwide Tour player, down on his luck and ready to quit the game in 2003, was loaned $3,000 by Brenden Pappas to continue playing?

93

Who said, "I had a great deal of talent. But talent alone will only take you so far"?
A) Greg Norman   B) Lee Trevino
C) Gary Player   D) Tony Lema

94

What disease did Ben Crenshaw successfully fight in the 1980s?

95

What player made a return to the Champions Tour in 2004 after battling tonsil and tongue cancer?

$50

AMERICAN IMPRESSED

TOUR CARD
NUMBER   EXPIRES
867-5309   01/01/XX
BIRTHDATE
XX/XX/XX
SEX   WT.
M   XXX

PGA
TOUR

DENT, JIM
Jim Dent

91 *To give to someone in need*

92 *Chris Couch. He went on to win twice and earned his PGA TOUR card.*

93 *C) Gary Player, who in his drive for success has won throughout five decades*

94 *Graves disease, which causes a defect in the immune system, affects the thyroid gland, and can lead to heart failure. Fortunately for Crenshaw and other sufferers, although Graves is incurable, it can be treated.*

95 *Hubert Green*

96

What legendary golfer suffered injuries in
World War I—including the loss of an eye and metal
plates in his head and arm—and went on to win
the U.S. Open, Western Open, British Open,
and PGA Championship?
A) Ralph Guldahl   B) Tommy Armour
C) Macdonald Smith   D) Johnny Revolta

97

What winner of the 1999 FedEx St. Jude
Classic is legally blind in his left eye?

98

What player published
photos of his ongoing hip
surgery on his website?

99

What was Andrew Magee
talking about when he said,
"There are better ways to weaken
the grip on your left hand"?

100

What player was stung about a dozen times
by killer bees at the 1996 Nortel Open?
A) Phil Mickelson   B) Jim Gallagher Jr.
C) Keith Fergus   D) Brad Bryant

96 *B) Tommy Armour, who was also one of golf's most respected instructors*

97 *Ted Tryba*

98 *Greg Norman*

99 *A 1998 chainsaw accident in which he slipped and cut his left index finger*

100 *C) Keith Fergus. He managed to shoot a 67 in the third round, however, and eventually tied for 13th in the event.*

101

What former U.S. Open champion was struck by lightning as a young man in South Africa and battled a series of health-related problems as a result?

102

What happened to Jerry Heard, Lee Trevino, and Bobby Nichols at the 1975 Western Open?

103

What player performed CPR on his caddie, whose heart had stopped beating, during the 1999 Cialis Western Open?

104

What player was so engrossed in lining up a putt during the 2000 Q-school that he walked backward off the green and fell into the water?

105

Who made international headlines at THE PLAYERS Championship in 2004 when he accidentally knocked his marked ball into a water hazard—only to see a friend drop his pants, wade in, and retrieve the ball so the player could avoid a two-stroke penalty?

101 *Retief Goosen*

102 *They were struck by lightning.*

103 *John Maginnes, who somehow managed to regain his composure and shoot a 1-under 71*

104 *Cliff Kresge*

105 *Ian Poulter. Poulter earned an additional $21,000 because of the saved strokes and promised to reward his friend for the effort.*

What player changed into an Austin Powers costume on Halloween before completing the 18th hole during the 2003 Nationwide Tour Championship?

107

What player pushed commissioner Deane Beman and architect Pete Dye into the lake at No. 18 following his THE PLAYERS Championship victory in 1982?

108

What did Lee Trevino pull from his bag and toss at Jack Nicklaus prior to their playoff at the 1971 U.S. Open?
A) A rubber snake   B) A banana peel
C) A large foam golf ball in case Nicklaus "couldn't" hit a regular ball
D) A white flag so Nicklaus could later "surrender" victory

109

Which golfer once attended the National Hot Rod Association's driving school, won a hot-rod sprint, and had drag racer Bob Vandergriff Jr. caddie for him?
A) Jay Don Blake   B) Jay Haas
C) Kenny Perry   D) Bruce Lietzke

110

Which British player was the first winner of the Masters to serve haggis at the Champions Dinner?
A) Colin Montgomerie   B) Tony Jacklin
C) Sandy Lyle   D) Peter Alliss

106 *David Morland IV*

107 *Jerry Pate, who promptly dove in himself*

108 *A) A rubber snake, which Nicklaus had seen previously and knew was coming. Trevino ended up beating Nicklaus by three shots.*

109 *A) Jay Don Blake*

110 *C) Sandy Lyle*

111

What unusual prize did Fran Quinn win at the
1999 Omega PGA Championship for making a hole-in-one?
A) His weight in golf balls   B) His weight in whiskey
C) His height in $20 bills   D) His weight in caviar

112

What Champions Tour player can always be
found with a peanut butter sandwich in his bag?
A) George Archer   B) Dave Eichelberger
C) Al Geiberger   D) Walter Hall

113

Why did Jesper Parnevik begin
turning up the bill of his cap?
A) To get a tan
B) To create a sponsorship opportunity
C) To separate himself from the other golfers
D) To keep the bill from distracting him while putting

114

What nickname did Doug
Sanders earn for wearing
such outlandishly loud
golfing attire?

115

What player once said,
"If you're going to be in
the limelight, you might
as well dress like it"?
A) Jimmy Demaret
B) Doug Sanders
C) Payne Stewart
D) Jesper Parnevik

111 *B) His weight in whiskey—roughly 175 pounds*

112 *C) Al Geiberger, who endorsed Skippy peanut butter while playing on the PGA TOUR*

113 *A) To get a tan*

114 *Peacock of the Fairways*

115 *A) Jimmy Demaret*

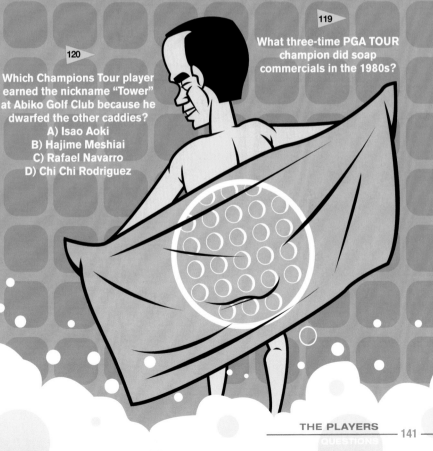

What Champions Tour player wears plus fours and socks with his name written down the side?

117 ►

The license plate on Darren Clarke's Ferrari reads "DC 60." What does it signify?

118 ►

Who was once a highly ranked tennis player in Nevada and spent five years working at Pizza Hut before playing on the PGA TOUR?

119 ►

What three-time PGA TOUR champion did soap commercials in the 1980s?

120 ►

Which Champions Tour player earned the nickname "Tower" at Abiko Golf Club because he dwarfed the other caddies?
A) Isao Aoki
B) Hajime Meshiai
C) Rafael Navarro
D) Chi Chi Rodriguez

116 *Rodger Davis*

117 *"DC 60" refers to his career low round.*

118 *Craig Barlow*

119 *Keith Fergus*

120 *A) Isao Aoki*

121

What was the name of
Payne Stewart, Mark Lye,
and Peter Jacobsen's band?

122

What band invited Shaun Micheel backstage
after he won the 2003 PGA Championship?
A) KISS B) Metallica C) AC/DC D) Ozzy Osbourne

123

What fan favorite and member of
the World Golf Hall of Fame once had
his picture used on a DEVO album?
A) Craig Stadler B) Peter Jacobsen
C) Chi Chi Rodriguez D) Lee Trevino

124

Who wrote and recorded the
biographical album "My Life"?
A) Payne Stewart B) Jason Gore
C) John Daly D) Fred Funk

125

Which of the following artists
contributed to "My Life"?
A) Darius Rucker B) Willie Nelson
C) Alice Cooper D) Both A and B

126

Who was Sam Snead talking about when
he said, "If [he] gave someone a blood
transfusion, the patient would freeze to death"?
A) Lloyd Mangrum B) Ralph Guldahl
C) Ben Hogan D) Tommy Bolt

ANSWERS

 121 *Jake Trout and the Flounders*

 122 *A) KISS*

 123 *C) Chi Chi Rodriguez*

 124 *C) John Daly, whose songs include "All My Exes Wear Rolexes"*

 125 *D) Both A and B*

126 *B) Ralph Guldahl, who played methodically and without emotion. Guldahl once said of himself, "Behind my so-called poker face, I'm burning up."*

What Champions Tour
player has an extensive
collection of Lionel Trains
and pinball machines?

What player earned the nickname
"Disco Dick" because he listened to
music in between holes?

Which of the following is true about Ken Green?
A) He once wrestled an alligator to save his dog.
B) He once bowled a 300.
C) He has won in the United States,
   Morocco, and Hong Kong.
D) All of the above

What two-time U.S. Amateur
Public Links champion was given his first
set of clubs by a priest in Los Angeles?

David Frost has produced a line
of wines in which every vintage is
named after a golfer. Who has
been featured on the bottles?
A) Gene Sarazen   B) Bobby Jones
C) Harry Vardon   D) None of the above

127 *Ed Dougherty*

128 *Richard Zokol*

129 *D) All of the above*

130 *David Berganio Jr.*

131 *A) Gene Sarazen. Sam Snead and Arnold Palmer have also been featured on Frost's wine bottles.*

132

Which player began writing a Bible verse on his ball so he could easily identify it after being penalized for hitting the wrong ball during a tournament?
A) Paul Azinger   B) Pat Bates
C) Kermit Zarley   D) Payne Stewart

133

Which player's golf balls are marked each week with messages and reminders from his wife and children?

134

What Champions Tour player and former Masters winner has marked his ball with an English half penny since 1969?

135

What winner of the 2001 JELD-WEN Tradition always keeps a penny in his pocket for good luck?
A) Gil Morgan   B) Jim Thorpe
C) Tom Watson   D) Doug Tewell

136

What Champions Tour player uses only white-colored tees and carries three coins—two pennies and a quarter—in his pocket?

132 **B) Pat Bates, an active member of the Fellowship of Christian Athletes**

133 **Duffy Waldorf**

134 **Charles Coody. The penny was a gift from his daughter Caryn.**

135 **D) Doug Tewell**

136 **Dave Barr**

137

Chi Chi Rodriguez has a unique tradition of marking his birdie putts and par putts. What is his ritual?

138

Which player is superstitious about not wanting to know in advance what players he'll be competing against during a tournament?
A) Ben Crane   B) Ben Curtis   C) Rich Beem   D) Todd Hamilton

139

Which Argentinean player walks to a religious shrine near his hometown after every victory?
A) Roberto De Vicenzo   B) José Coceres
C) Angel Cabrera   D) Ricardo Gonzalez

140

The distinguished British golf writer Pat Ward-Thomas once wrote, "I never saw a golfer who seemed so assured of his destiny. There is about him the unmistakable air of success." Who was he describing?

141

Who was the first Canadian to be inducted into the World Golf Hall of Fame?

137 *He marks his birdie putts with a quarter and his par putts with a nickel. The coin is always heads up.*

138 *A) Ben Crane. He says he doesn't want to go to sleep thinking about it, since many of the golfers he competes with are people he once watched on TV.*

139 *B) José Coceres*

140 *Peter Thomson, who won nearly 60 tournaments worldwide, including three consecutive British Opens*

141 *Marlene Stewart Streit, who maintained her amateur status throughout her career and is the only golfer to have won the Australian, British, Canadian, and United States women's amateur championships*

142

Which two-time Masters champion
is a Player Ambassador for the
World Golf Hall of Fame?
A) Nick Faldo
B) Bernhard Langer
C) Seve Ballesteros
D) Ben Crenshaw

143

Which American players were named honorary members
of the Royal & Ancient Golf Club of St. Andrews?
A) Gene Sarazen, Jack Nicklaus, and Tom Watson
B) Arnold Palmer, Tiger Woods, and Tom Kite
C) Tom Watson, Tiger Woods, and Arnold Palmer
D) Both A and B

144

What year did Ken Venturi serve as
an honorary starter at the Masters?

145

What royal honor do Nick Faldo,
Graham Marsh, and Sam Torrance
have in common?

146

Which player can trace his lineage to Scotland's
royal Robert the Bruce (King of Bannockburn)?

142 *D) Ben Crenshaw*

143 *A) Gene Sarazen, Jack Nicklaus, and Tom Watson*

144 *1983*

145 *They are Members of the British Empire.*

146 *Geoff Ogilvy*

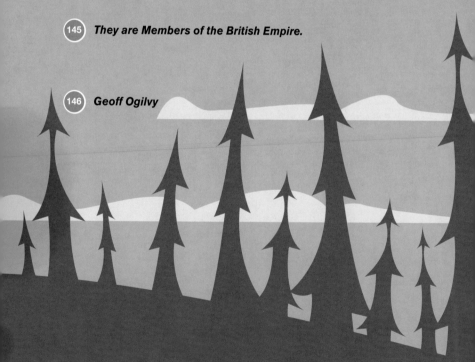

Who was Gene Sarazen talking about when he said,
"[He] is the only person who came into the game
possessing every physical attribute–a sound swing,
power, a sturdy physique, and no bad habits"?
A) Bobby Jones   B) Jack Nicklaus
C) Arnold Palmer   D) Sam Snead

Which of the following is true about Bobby Lincoln?
A) He never played competitive golf as an amateur.
B) He designed himself a putter based on a gun barrel.
C) He has made holes-in-one with both a right-handed
and left-handed swing.
D) Both A and B

Who is known as
golf's "Iron Man"?

Which player has been known
to putt right- or left-handed, depending
on the direction the putt breaks?
A) Notah Begay III   B) Adam Scott
C) Stewart Cink   D) Jerry Kelly

True or false: Outside
of golf Phil Mickelson
is right-handed.

147 *D) Sam Snead. He is considered by many to have had the smoothest, most natural swing ever.*

148 *D) Both A and B*

149 *Dana Quigley, who breaks his own Champions Tour record for consecutive starts every time he tees it up*

150 *A) Notah Begay III*

151 *True. Mickelson learned the game by mirroring his dad's right-handed teachings.*

152

As a child, which left-handed golfer wrote to Jack Nicklaus asking for advice on whether he should switch to playing right-handed?
A) Phil Mickelson   B) Steve Flesch
C) Bob Charles   D) Mike Weir

153

Whose father was the national left-handed champ in 1965?
A) Phil Blackmar   B) Mike Weir
C) Steve Flesch   D) Phil Mickelson

154

What self-taught player once said, "There's nobody who could teach my swing"?

155

Who was Sam Snead talking about when he said, "He could get the ball up and down from a manhole"?

156

What Champions Tour player and former college hockey star has used only two putters in his career?

157

Why was Ben Hogan's victory at the 1950 U.S. Open so significant?

152 *D) Mike Weir. Nicklaus wrote back and told him to stick
to his natural swing.*

153 *A) Phil Blackmar's father, Fred. Blackmar himself, a
right-hander, has won three PGA TOUR events.*

154 Jonathan Kaye

155 *Paul Runyan, who had one of golf's finest short games.
Runyan believed that on pitch shots, a golfer should not hold
the club any farther up the shaft than necessary. He preached
control around the green and believed the best way to obtain
it was to choke down on the club.*

156 *Allen Doyle*

157 *One year before, in 1949, Hogan had been in a
life-threatening auto accident when a Greyhound bus
crashed into his car. His comeback is one of the most
famous and inspiring in all of golf.*

What Australian golfer won the Golf Writers
Association of America's Ben Hogan Award in 2001
after recovering from a traffic accident that left
him with a broken sternum and facial injuries?
A) Greg Norman   B) Stuart Appleby
C) Robert Allenby   D) Craig Parry

159

Who was Lanny Wadkins referring to when he
said: "[He] would never tolerate a weakness.
He'd go to the practice tee and beat at it until
the darn thing went away"?
A) Tiger Woods   B) Tom Watson
C) Johnny Miller   D) Ben Crenshaw

160

Which golfer completed the 2001 White Rock
Marathon in Dallas in less than four hours?
A) Tom Kite   B) Justin Leonard
C) Joel Edwards   D) Bob Estes

161

Who first played golf on Easter
Sunday in 1978, and then, 18
years later on Easter, won his
first PGA TOUR event at the
1996 BellSouth Classic?

162

Name the hard-luck player who needed
a par on the final hole of the 2001
Q-school to earn his PGA TOUR card,
but had his ball bounce off a cart path
and land on the clubhouse roof. His
subsequent drop landed in an unplayable
lie and he wound up with a triple bogey.

158 *C) Robert Allenby*

159 *B) Tom Watson, whose legendary determination allowed him to become one of the game's greatest champions*

160 *B) Justin Leonard*

161 *Paul Stankowski*

162 *Roland Thatcher*

163

Gil Morgan made a hole-in-one once during the PGA Championship that caused a 15-minute delay. What happened?

164

Which golfer was the first since 1938 to sweep all the female amateur championships, winning the Trans-Amateur Championship, Western Amateur Championship, and U.S. Amateur Championship in 1998?
A) Gloria Park   B) Jenny Park-Choi   C) Grace Park   D) Se Ri Pak

165

Which female player is the only golfer to win the British Women's Amateur and U.S. Women's Amateur in the same year?
A) Annika Sorenstam   B) Karrie Webb
C) Kelli Kuehne   D) Natalie Gulbis

166

Who was Bobby Jones talking about when he said, "When [he] saw a chance at the bacon hanging over the last green, he could put as much fire and fury into a finishing round as Jack Dempsey could put into a fight"?
A) Gene Sarazen   B) Sam Snead
C) Paul Runyan   D) Horton Smith

167

What player has the most professional tournament titles in history?

(163) His ball went in the hole on the fly and tore out part of the cup, which officials had to repair.

(164) C) Grace Park. By the end of the 2004 season, she had won six LPGA events, including a major championship.

(165) C) Kelli Kuehne, whose brother is Hank Kuehne, one of the PGA TOUR's longest drivers

(166) A) Gene Sarazen, whose late-round heroics included making birdie on the final hole of his first U.S. Open at age 20 to win

(167) Kathy Whitworth, who has earned 88 titles, including six major championships

BUNKER SHOT

MATCH THE FOLLOWING PLAYERS WITH THEIR CORRECT NICKNAME:

Miguel Angel Jimenez	The Merry Mex
Isao Aoki	The Bulldog
Miller Barber	Dr. Dirt
Ed Fiori	Little Poison
Graham Marsh	Boss of the Moss
Hajime Meshiai	The Mechanic
Mike Reid	Lighthorse
Craig Stadler	Champagne
Brad Bryant	Radar
Paul Runyan	Popeye
Tony Lema	Swampy
Shigeki Maruyama	El Gato
Lee Trevino	The Smiling Assassin
Tommy Armour III	The Silver Scot
Craig Parry	Mr. X
Loren Roberts	Tower
Gene Sarazen	The Grip
Eduardo Romero	The Walrus
Corey Pavin	The Squire
Harry Cooper	Kong

BUNKER SHOT

ANSWERS:

Miguel Angel Jimenez: The Mechanic

Isao Aoki: Tower

Miller Barber: Mr. X

Ed Fiori: The Grip

Graham Marsh: Swampy

Hajime Meshiai: Kong

Mike Reid: Radar

Craig Stadler: The Walrus

Brad Bryant: Dr. Dirt

Paul Runyan: Little Poison

Tony Lema: Champagne

Shigeki Maruyama: The Smiling Assassin

Lee Trevino: The Merry Mex

Tommy Armour III: The Silver Scot

Craig Parry: Popeye

Loren Roberts: Boss of the Moss

Gene Sarazen: The Squire

Eduardo Romero: El Gato

Corey Pavin: The Bulldog

Harry Cooper: Lighthorse

RECORDS
of Aces and Snowmen

**It took me 17 years to get 3,000 hits in baseball.
I did it in one afternoon on the golf course.**

– HANK AARON –

1

How many total major championships did Bobby Jones win from 1923 until his retirement at age 28 in 1930?
A) 7 B) 9 C) 11 D) 13

2

How many times did Jug McSpaden finish in the top 10 in 1945 to set the PGA TOUR record?
A) 21 B) 31 C) 41 D) None of the above

3

How many official PGA TOUR events did Byron Nelson win in 1945?
A) 11 B) 15 C) 18 D) 21

4

Since 1970, five players have won seven or more times in one year on the PGA TOUR. Who are they?

5

Who owns the all-time record for the most consecutive PGA TOUR victories?
A) Ben Hogan B) Byron Nelson
C) Tiger Woods D) Jack Nicklaus

6

How many total major championships—both amateur and professional—has Jack Nicklaus won?
A) 16 B) 18 C) 20 D) 22

1 **D) 13. This ranks second only to Jack Nicklaus's 20 major wins (including two amateurs), which occurred over a span of 27 years.**

2 **B) 31 times**

3 **C) 18–five better than any other player's best single season**

4 **Jack Nicklaus (1972, 1973), Johnny Miller (1974), Tom Watson (1980), Tiger Woods (1999, 2000), and Vijay Singh (2004)**

5 **B) Byron Nelson, who won 11 straight victories in 1945**

6 **C) 20. He won six Masters, four U.S. Opens, three British Opens, five PGA Championships, and two U.S. Amateurs.**

7

Who has the most top-10
career finishes at 358?
A) Byron Nelson   B) Jug McSpaden
C) Billy Casper   D) Sam Snead

8

Who won 10 or more times during
two separate seasons?

9

What player had the most longevity, winning his
final PGA TOUR event nearly 29 years after his first?
A) Ray Floyd   B) Sam Snead
C) Tom Watson   D) Jack Nicklaus

10

Two players share the record
for going the most years–17–with at
least one victory. Who are they?
A) Byron Nelson and Sam Snead
B) Byron Nelson and Ben Hogan
C) Jack Nicklaus and Arnold Palmer
D) Jack Nicklaus and Sam Snead

11

What was Arnold Palmer's
longest consecutive winning
streak during any one season
of his PGA TOUR career?
A) Three   B) Five
C) Seven   D) Nine

12

What Champions Tour player owns the record
for most consecutive victories in a season?
A) Hale Irwin   B) Lee Trevino
C) Bob Charles   D) Chi Chi Rodriguez

13

Name the only player to win more
than three times in a single season
on the Nationwide Tour.

7 *D) Sam Snead*

8 *Ben Hogan, who had 13 victories in 1946 and 10 in 1948*

9 *A) Ray Floyd, who won the first of his 22 titles in 1963 and the last in 1992*

10 *C) Jack Nicklaus (1962 to 1978) and Arnold Palmer (1955 to 1971)*

11 *A) Three. Palmer achieved this milestone in both 1960 and 1962.*

12 *D) Chi Chi Rodriguez, who won four in a row in 1987, the same season Bob Charles won three consecutive tournaments*

13 *Sean Murphy. He won four times during the 1993 season, four years before the Battlefield Promotion went into effect.*

14

What former Nationwide Tour player
has the most wins on the PGA TOUR?

15

Where do Billy Casper's 51 PGA TOUR
wins rank him on the all-time list?

16

How many wins separate Sam Snead from
runner-up Jack Nicklaus on the all-time
PGA TOUR victory list?

17

Which player is second on the list for winning
the most professional majors in his career?
A) Walter Hagen   B) Gary Player
C) Ben Hogan   D) Tiger Woods

18

How many times has Jack Nicklaus
finished in the top 10 on the money list?
A) 13   B) 18   C) 20   D) 22

19

Who owns the record for the biggest
single-season jump in earnings?

20

What two players led the
PGA TOUR money list for the
most consecutive years?
A) Tiger Woods and Jack Nicklaus
B) Greg Norman and Fred Couples
C) Tiger Woods and Greg Norman
D) Tiger Woods and Tom Watson

14 *Ernie Els, whose three wins in 2004 brought his total to 15, two ahead of David Duval*

15 *At number six, behind Sam Snead, Jack Nicklaus, Ben Hogan, Arnold Palmer, and Byron Nelson*

16 *Nine wins. Snead owns 82 and Nicklaus, 73.*

17 *A) Walter Hagen, who won 11 career professional major championships, seven fewer than first-place winner, Jack Nicklaus*

18 *B) 18 times, three more times than runner-up Sam Snead*

19 *Tiger Woods. In 1999, he netted $4,775,468 more than in 1998.*

20 *D) Tiger Woods and Tom Watson both led the list for four years, from 1999 to 2002 and 1977 to 1980, respectively.*

21

In 2004, a record 77 players passed the $1 million mark in season earnings–and several more were close to that number. Which group just missed hitting seven figures?
A) Ryan Palmer, Briny Baird, and Ben Crane
B) Stephen Leaney, Tim Clark, and Vaughn Taylor
C) Loren Roberts, Shaun Micheel, and Bernhard Langer
D) None of the above

22

What record did David Toms set in 2002 when he won a season total of $3,459,740?

23

During Byron Nelson's record run in 1945, he claimed 11 consecutive victories. What was the most he won in any single event?
A) $1,000   B) $3,000
C) $5,000   D) $10,000

24

What two players have led the Champions Tour money list for the greatest number of years?
A) Hale Irwin and Gil Morgan
B) Hale Irwin and Lee Trevino
C) Hale Irwin and Don January
D) Bruce Fleisher and Lee Trevino

25

Which player owns the best single-season scoring average on the Champions Tour?

26

Which player replaced Tiger Woods atop the Official World Golf Ranking in 1999 and ended his run of 41 consecutive weeks?

21 C) *Loren Roberts, Shaun Micheel, and Bernhard Langer. Roberts was closest at $998,677.*

22 *Toms won the most money in a season without claiming a title. He finished second three times, though.*

23 D) *$10,000, the first-place prize at the Tam O'Shanter Open in Chicago*

24 C) *Hale Irwin (1997, 1998, and 2002) and Don January (1980, 1983, and 1984)*

25 *Hale Irwin. In 1998, Irwin scored a 68.59 and won seven times.*

26 *David Duval, who held the title for 14 weeks*

27

How many of the 10 lowest non-adjusted scoring averages can Jack Nicklaus claim?
A) One B) Two C) Three
D) None of the above

28

In 1945, Byron Nelson shot a record-setting non-adjusted scoring average–a record that stood until Tiger Woods broke it in 2000. What was Nelson's average?

29

How many of the top five best single-season non-adjusted scoring averages belong to Tiger Woods?
A) Two B) Three C) Four D) Five

30

Tiger Woods has the best non-adjusted scoring average in history. What was his record-setting total in 2000?

31

At the 2004 Deutsche Bank Championship, Vijay Singh overtook Tiger Woods on the Official World Golf Ranking. How many consecutive weeks had Woods held on to the No. 1 spot?

32

Where was Ben Curtis on the Official World Golf Ranking when he stunned the golfing world and won the British Open in 2003?

33

At what 2004 tournament did Tiger Woods aim to set the record for most consecutive victories in a single event?
A) the Memorial Tournament
B) World Golf Championships–American Express Championship
C) Bay Hill Invitational
D) World Golf Championships–NEC Invitational

27 *D) None of the above. Though Nicklaus is one of golf's most talented players, he doesn't own any of the 10 lowest scoring averages.*

28 *Nelson scored a 68.34. He did not receive the Vardon Trophy, though—it was not awarded that year because of World War II.*

29 *B) Three. Woods owns the three lowest averages, which he scored beginning in 2000. Davis Love III and Vijay Singh round out the top five.*

30 *68.17*

31 *He had been at No. 1 for 264 weeks. Woods fell to No. 3, behind Ernie Els, a short time later.*

32 *No. 396*

33 *C) Bay Hill Invitational, where his run came up short after his joint 46th*

34
Which golfer owns the record outright for most victories in a single PGA TOUR event?
A) Sam Snead B) "Young" Tom Morris
C) Gene Sarazen D) Tiger Woods

35
How many successive U.S. Amateur championships did Tiger Woods win?
A) Two B) Three C) Four D) Five

36
Name the only player to win the U.S. Amateur, NCAA Championship, U.S. Public Links, and Western Amateur in the same year.

37
Who is the youngest amateur winner of a PGA TOUR event in history?
A) Francis Ouimet
B) Chick Evans
C) Phil Mickelson
D) None of the above

38
What PGA TOUR star owns the Nationwide Tour record for best finish by an amateur?

39
How many victories in a single event has Hale Irwin won on the Champions Tour?
A) Four B) Five C) Six
D) None of the above

34 *A) Sam Snead, who never won more than two of his record number of Greater Greensboro Open victories in succession*

35 *B) Three*

36 *Ryan Moore, from the University of Nevada–Las Vegas. He had a 2004 season that has been called "the most amazing amateur season since Bobby Jones in 1930."*

37 *B) Chick Evans, who won the 1910 Western Open at 20 years, 1 month, and 15 days. The second-youngest winner, Francis Ouimet, was 20 years, 4 months, and 12 days old.*

38 *Charles Howell III. He tied for second at the 2000 Greensboro Open and then turned professional the following week.*

39 *B) Six. He won the 1997 and 2000 Kaanapali Classic and won the tournament–renamed the Turtle Bay Championship after a sponsor change–again in 2001, 2002, 2003, and 2005, giving him the record for number of tournament wins.*

40

How many titles did Sam Snead claim at the Greater Greensboro Open?
A) Five B) Seven C) Nine
D) None of the above

41

Sam Snead's record-breaking wins at the Greater Greensboro Open were spaced record-breaking years apart. How many years were sandwiched between his first and last wins?
A) 22 B) 27 C) 29 D) 30

42

How many years did Dick Mast go between Nationwide Tour victories?
A) Five B) Seven C) Eight D) Nine

43

What player went 15 years between PGA TOUR victories, marking the longest drought between titles?

44

How many events did Joey Sindelar compete in between his victories at the 1990 Hardees Golf Classic and the 2004 Wachovia Championship?

45

Which player entered the 2005 season with the record for the most Nationwide Tour starts in his career?
A) R. W. Eaks B) John Elliott
C) Steve Haskins D) Ben Bates

46

Which player went 28 years between his last win on the PGA TOUR and his first win on the Champions Tour?
A) Billy Casper B) Miller Barber
C) Gary Player D) Mike Fetchick

40 **D) None of the above.** Snead won eight in all–the record for the most victories in a single event.

41 **B) 27 years.** Snead won his first title in 1938 and his eighth in 1965.

42 **D) Nine years** spanned his 1990 Fort Wayne Open title and his 1999 New Mexico Classic crown.

43 **Butch Baird, who had 240 starts between his 1961 and 1976 wins**

44 **370**

45 **C) Steve Haskins, who has won twice in those 358 starts**

46 **D) Mike Fetchick.** He won the Mayfair Inn Open in 1956, but didn't score another victory until 1985, when he claimed the Hilton Head Seniors International.

47

What player put together the
biggest come-from-behind victory
in Champions Tour history?

48

John Flannery and Gary Hallberg both own the
Nationwide Tour record for the best come-from-behind
victory. How many strokes did they overcome?

49

Who scored the largest come-from-behind victory
in a major championship by rebounding from 10
strokes back to win the 1999 British Open?
A) Jean Van de Velde   B) Justin Leonard
C) Tom Lehman   D) Paul Lawrie

50

What record did Mike Souchak set when
he won the 1956 St. Paul Open?

51

What record did Bob Goalby set
at the 1961 St. Petersburg Open?

52

Joe Durant made a record number
of birdies when he won the 2001 Bob
Hope Chrysler Classic. How many did he
accumulate during the 90-hole event?
A) 17   B) 27   C) 37   D) 47

47 *Jay Sigel. He earned his first professional victory at the 1994 GTE West Classic by overcoming a 10-stroke deficit to tie Jim Colbert in regulation before defeating him in a playoff.*

48 *10*

49 *D) Paul Lawrie*

50 *He birdied his last six holes to win—the most consecutive birdies to win a tournament in PGA TOUR history.*

51 *Goalby was the first player to birdie eight in a row. Five other players have since tied that record, but of those golfers, only Goalby and Fuzzy Zoeller went on to win their respective tournaments.*

52 *C) 37, roughly 41 percent of his holes. Phil Mickelson tied that number at the 2004 event.*

53

What Nationwide Tour player has made the most birdies in a row?
A) Tom Lehman   B) Omar Uresti   C) Bob May   D) Rocky Walcher

54

What two players own the best birdie-eagle streak in history, with seven birdies and one eagle?

55

In 2001, Mark Calcavecchia and Paul Gow each collected a record number of birdies during a 72-hole event. How many did they make?

56

At the 2003 Mercedes Championships, Ernie Els defeated K. J. Choi and Rocco Mediate by eight strokes. What record did he set with his score of 261?

57

Which of the following players did not lower the record for the most strokes under par after 72 holes?
A) Ben Hogan   B) Mike Souchak
C) John Huston   D) Joe Durant

58

For more than 45 years, the PGA TOUR's 72-hole scoring record was unbreakable after being set at 257 at the 1955 Texas Open. Who held this title for all those years?

53 *B) Omar Uresti, who sank nine straight at the 1994 Shreveport Open, which he went on to win. Uresti's record beats any on the PGA TOUR, Champions Tour, and European Tour.*

54 *Billy Mayfair (during the final round of the 2001 Buick Open) and Briny Baird (during the second round of the 2003 FUNAI Classic at the Walt Disney World Resort)*

55 *Thirty-two. Calcavecchia scored his birdies during his win at the 2001 Phoenix Open. Gow, however, lost in a playoff to Jeff Sluman at the B.C. Open.*

56 *Els set the record for the most strokes under par: 31-under on the par-73 Plantation Course.*

57 *B) Mike Souchak. He tied Ben Hogan's mark of 27-under in 1955, but didn't better it.*

58 *Mike Souchak. Souchak was watching the Phoenix Open on television when Mark Calcavecchia broke his record, posting a 256.*

A

In 1978, Walter Zembriski, who has since gone on to win three Champions Tour titles, set me when he played the Cherry Hills layout in a mere two hours, 13 minutes.
What record am I?

B

Sam Snead set me when he competed in the Manufacturers Hanover Westchester Classic in 1979. What record am I?

C

Gary Player achieved me after claiming roughly 15 million of these–a milestone that has nothing to do with Masters titles, U.S. Opens, or victories of any kind.
What record am I?

D

Jack Nicklaus, Ben Hogan, and Tiger Woods each set me, joining a short list of golf's greats when they won the British Open. What prestigious record am I?

E

Golfing icon Arnold Palmer achieved me in 1976, but it took him a long time to do so–57 hours, 25 minutes, and 42 seconds to be exact. What record am I?

WHAT RECORD AM I?

WHAT RECORD AM I?

(A) **The fastest round in U.S. Open history**

(B) **The record for the oldest player to make a cut on the PGA TOUR**

(C) **The record for the world's most traveled athlete at 15 million miles**

(D) **The Career Grand Slam**

(E) **The aviation record for circumnavigating the globe in a Lear 36**

59 ▶

Mark Calcavecchia's 72-hole scoring record in 2001 didn't stand for nearly as long as his predecessor's. Who went lower by two strokes at the 2003 Valero Texas Open?

60 ▶

Al Geiberger, Chip Beck, and David Duval have all shot 59s on the PGA TOUR. Of these three, which player needed to make an eagle putt on his final hole to reach the magic number?

61 ▶

Which of the three players listed above did not go on to win the tournament, despite his incredible score?

62 ▶

What did Jason Bohn shoot to win the Canadian Tour's 2001 Bayer Championship?

63 ▶

Who scored a nine-hole record of 27 on the PGA TOUR?
A) Mike Souchak   B) Andy North
C) Billy Mayfair   D) All of the above

64 ▶

Which player holds the record for fewest putts in nine holes?
A) Sam Trahan   B) Kenny Knox
C) John Inman   D) Stan Utley

65 ▶

What is the Champions Tour record for the lowest nine-hole score?
A) 27   B) 28   C) 29
D) None of the above

59 *Tommy Armour III, who earned his first victory in 164 months and 366 starts*

60 *David Duval*

61 *Chip Beck, who finished tied for third at the 1991 Las Vegas Invitational. David Duval won the 1999 Bob Hope Chrysler Classic by a stroke, while Al Geiberger won the 1977 Memphis Classic by three strokes.*

62 *Fifty-eight, the lowest round ever recorded on that tour in competition*

63 *D) All of the above. Mike Souchak first set the record at the 1955 Texas Open. Andy North later tied him at the 1975 B.C. Open, and Billy Mayfair joined the group at the 2001 Buick Open. Robert Gamez made it a foursome by hitting that number at the 2004 Bob Hope Chrysler Classic.*

64 *D) Stan Utley, who used just six putts on the front nine during the second round of the 2002 Air Canada Championship*

65 *A) 27. Both Jay Sigel and Seiji Ebihara have recorded this score.*

66
Which player owns the lowest consecutive 36-hole mark in PGA TOUR history at 124?

67
Tiger Woods, Mark Calcavecchia, and Tom Lehman share the record for the lowest opening 36-hole score, at 125. Which player had the most strokes under par?

68
Six players share the fewest putts in one round, at 18. Who first set the PGA TOUR record?
A) Mike McGee B) Kenny Knox
C) Andy North D) Sam Trahan

69
After making 18 putts in the first round of the 1989 MCI Heritage Classic, Kenny Knox was on his way to setting the PGA TOUR record for the fewest putts in four rounds. What was his final number?
A) 90 B) 93 C) 95 D) 96

70
Each of the players below holds the record for the lowest opening 54 holes. Which one achieved this on a par-70 course?
A) John Cook B) Mark Calcavecchia
C) Tommy Armour III D) Both A and B

71
Who was the first player to set a new low for opening 54 holes in a tournament, scoring 191?

66 *Mark Calcavecchia, who shot 60-64 in the second and third rounds of the 2001 Phoenix Open. He eventually won the tournament over Rocco Mediate by eight strokes.*

67 *Tom Lehman, who shot a 62-63 on par-72 courses to stand 19 under. Calcavecchia was 17-under on a par-71 course, while Woods was 15-under on a par-70 course.*

68 *D) Sam Trahan, in the final round of the 1979 IVB Philadelphia Golf Classic*

69 *B) 93. This number was later tied by Mark Calcavecchia at the 2002 Greater Greensboro Chrysler Classic.*

70 *C) Tommy Armour III, who had rounds of 64-62-63 to start the 2003 Valero Texas Open at The Resort at LaCantera*

71 *Johnny Palmer. Palmer's 1954 record stood for 42 years until John Cook went two lower at the 1996 FedEx St. Jude Classic.*

72

Name the only player to close out the final
54 holes in a PGA TOUR event with a 189.

73

Which Champions Tour player owns
the lowest 54-hole score at 191?
A) Allen Doyle   B) Bruce Fleisher
C) Hale Irwin   D) Tom Kite

74

Who shot rounds of 65-61-67-66-65 to
set the 90-hole scoring record of 324?

75

The lowest nine 90-hole scores
ever recorded on the PGA TOUR range
between 324 and 329. How many have
included at least one round in the 70s?

76

Which Champions Tour player shot the
most consecutive sub-70 rounds in a season?
A) Hale Irwin   B) Bruce Fleisher
C) Ray Floyd   D) Lee Trevino

72 *Chandler Harper, who finished with three consecutive 63s to beat Johnny Palmer by two strokes at the 1954 Texas Open. Incidentally, it was the same tournament in which Palmer opened his first 54 holes with a 191.*

73 *B) Bruce Fleisher, who shot rounds of 60-64-67 at the 2002 RJR Championship*

74 *Joe Durant. Durant beat Paul Stankowski by four strokes at the 2001 Bob Hope Chrysler Classic.*

75 *One. D. A. Weibring scored a 70 in the opening round of the 1991 Las Vegas Invitational. He eventually lost the event in a playoff to Andrew Magee.*

76 *A) Hale Irwin, who had 13 such rounds in 1999. Of those rounds, he won twice, lost twice in playoffs, and tied once for third.*

77

What player scored the most consecutive rounds at par or better during the 2000 and 2001 seasons?

78

Which player has recorded the longest drive on the PGA TOUR since 1980, the first year official stats were kept?
A) John Daly   B) Hank Kuehne   C) Chris Smith   D) Davis Love III

79

Which World Golf Hall of Famer made the most cuts in his PGA TOUR career?
A) Ray Floyd   B) Tom Kite
C) Jack Nicklaus   D) Arnold Palmer

80

By the end of the 2004 season, Tiger Woods had extended his streak of consecutive cuts to a record 133. Who stands second on the all-time list?

81

Which of the following players went on to win a Nationwide Tour event after making the cut exactly on the number?
A) Doug Martin   B) Stan Utley
C) Tripp Isenhour   D) All of the above

82

Which player entered the final round of a tournament 13 strokes ahead, the largest lead ever?
A) Bobby Locke   B) Tiger Woods
C) Gene Sarazen   D) Walter Hagen

77 *Tiger Woods. He went on to win six times during that span.*

78 *D) Davis Love III, who shot a 476-yarder at the 2004 Mercedes Championships*

79 *B) Tom Kite made 587 cuts, holding a slim edge over Ray Floyd's 583.*

80 *Byron Nelson comes in a distant second at 113.*

81 *D) All of the above. Doug Martin did so at the 1993 South Texas Open, Stan Utley at the 1995 Louisiana Open, and Tripp Isenhour at the 2000 Mississippi Gulf Coast Classic. Justin Bolli joined that group in 2004 at the Chattanooga Classic.*

82 *A) Bobby Locke earned this record at the 1948 Chicago Victory National Championship. He went on to win by 16 strokes.*

83

What dubious distinction do Greg Norman, Hal Sutton, Gay Brewer, and Bobby Cruickshank all share?

84

How many strokes were J. D. Edgar, Joe Kirkwood Sr., and Bobby Locke each up to hold the record for the largest winning margin?
A) 15   B) 16   C) 17   D) 18

85

Which player scored the largest winning margin at a major championship?
A) Jack Nicklaus   B) Ben Hogan
C) Tiger Woods   D) Gene Sarazen

86

At the 1997 Omaha Classic, Chris Smith set the record for the largest winning margin in a Nationwide Tour event. How many strokes was he up?
A) 8   B) 11   C) 13   D) 14

87

Who is the youngest professional to shoot his age or better in a PGA TOUR event?

83 *They share the record for having the largest lead with 18 holes to play–six strokes–yet going on to lose their respective tournaments.*

84 *B) 16*

85 *C) Tiger Woods, who won by 15 strokes at the 2000 U.S. Open. He also scored the second-largest margin with his 12-stroke victory at the 1997 Masters.*

86 *B) Smith was up by 11 strokes, setting two additional Nationwide Tour records–for most strokes under par at 26 and best 72-hole score at 258.*

87 *Sam Snead. At age 67, he scored a 66-67 at the 1979 Quad Cities Open.*

88

What is the largest winning margin
in a 54-hole Champions Tour event?
A) 7 strokes   B) 9 strokes
C) 10 strokes   D) 12 strokes

89

Name the oldest player to shoot lower than
his age in a Champions Tour event.
A) Jug McSpaden   B) Jack Fleck
C) Fred Haas   D) Gary Player

90

Who was the youngest player to
make a cut on the PGA TOUR?
A) Ty Tryon   B) Francis Ouimet
C) Bob Panasik   D) Tommy Jacobs

91

Who was the youngest player to
make a cut on the Nationwide Tour?
A) Michelle Wie   B) Sean Harlingten
C) Sean O'Hair   D) David Duval

92

What two-time Masters winner
scored the most PGA TOUR
victories before his 21st birthday?

93

Who is the oldest winner in
Nationwide Tour history?

88 *B) 9 strokes. Three Champions Tour players have hit this record, most recently Dave Stockton at the 1993 Franklin Quest Championship.*

89 *A) Jug McSpaden. At age 85, McSpaden shot an 81 at the 1994 PGA Seniors' Championship.*

90 *C) Bob Panasik. He was just 15 years old at the 1957 Bell Canadian Open.*

91 *B) Sean Harlingten, who was 16 years old at the 2003 Mark Christopher Charity Classic. He fired rounds of 69-69-72-69 to finish tied for 33rd.*

92 *Horton Smith, who earned seven victories*

93 *Dick Mast, who won the 1999 New Mexico Classic at age 48*

94

Who is the youngest winner in the PGA TOUR record books?

95

Name the oldest U.S. player to earn a Ryder Cup berth.

96

Which player won 42 times in his 30s, setting the record for the most titles won by a golfer in his fourth decade?
A) Ben Hogan   B) Arnold Palmer
C) Jack Nicklaus   D) Sam Snead

97

Which player won a record 17 times after the age of 40?

98

Why did John Barnum enter the record books when he won the 1962 Cajun Classic at age 51?
A) He became the only player over 50 to win on the PGA TOUR.
B) He became the oldest first-time winner.
C) He became the oldest player to win in his first start.
D) None of the above

99

What is the record for the greatest number of players involved in a PGA TOUR playoff?
A) 6   B) 8   C) 9   D) 10

100

The 1988 PGA TOUR season saw a record number of playoffs, breaking a longstanding record from 1972. How many playoffs were there?
A) 12   B) 15   C) 16   D) 21

94 *John McDermott. He was two months shy of his 20th birthday when he won the 1911 U.S. Open.*

95 *Fred Funk. He landed a spot on the team in 2004 at age 48.*

96 *B) Arnold Palmer, who won 42 of his 62 PGA TOUR titles during that time*

97 *Sam Snead*

98 *B) He became the oldest first-time winner.*

99 *A) 6 players. This has happened twice, most recently at the 2001 Nissan Open. Robert Allenby won when, on the first hole, he knocked a 3-wood through freezing rain to land within five feet for a birdie.*

100 *C) 16. This number was later matched in 1991, breaking the previous 1972 record by one.*

101

How many holes was the 1998 Lehigh Valley Open playoff, the longest sudden-death playoff in Nationwide Tour history?

102

Which Nationwide Tour season was deemed the "Year of the Playoff"?

103

Which player won the longest sudden-death playoff in Champions Tour history in 1998?
A) Dave Stockton   B) Gil Morgan
C) Bob Murphy   D) David Graham

104

What was the result of the 1949 Motor City Open sudden-death playoff, the longest in PGA TOUR history?
A) Cary Middlecoff won with an eagle.
B) Cary Middlecoff won with a double bogey.
C) Lloyd Mangrum was disqualified.
D) Both were deemed co-winners.

105

In 2002, the PGA TOUR record was set for the most first-time winners in a season. How many players entered the victory circle that year?

106

Ryan Palmer's win at the 2004 FUNAI Classic was the 159th win by a former Nationwide Tour player on the PGA TOUR, and it set a record for most wins in a season by former Nationwide Tour players. How many tournaments did they win?
A) 12   B) 15   C) 19   D) 22

101 *Nine holes. Eric Booker defeated Notah Begay III.*

102 *1991. That year, 13 events went into playoffs. This easily eclipsed the previous mark of nine, which also occurred in 1991 and later in 1998.*

103 *D) David Graham, who outlasted Dave Stockton after 10 holes at the Royal Caribbean Classic*

104 *D) Both Middlecoff and Mangrum were deemed co-winners after 11 playoff holes.*

105 *Eighteen—four more than the previous record set in 1991*

106 *D) 22. This broke the 2002 record of 21.*

BUNKER SHOT

MATCH THE PLAYERS BELOW WITH THEIR CORRECT NUMBER
OF CAREER PGA TOUR WINS (IN THE CASE WHERE TWO OR MORE
PLAYERS ARE TIED, JUST ONE PLAYER WITH THAT TOTAL IS LISTED):

Sam Snead	64
Jack Nicklaus	82
Ben Hogan	73
Arnold Palmer	51
Byron Nelson	29
Billy Casper	44
Walter Hagen	52
Cary Middlecoff	39
Gene Sarazen	62
Horton Smith	23
Harry Cooper	31
Leo Diegel	26
Lee Trevino	30
Henry Picard	25
Johnny Miller	22
Gary Player	21
Vijay Singh	32
Ray Floyd	20
Lanny Wadkins	24
Greg Norman	40

BUNKER SHOT

ANSWERS:

Sam Snead: 82

Jack Nicklaus: 73

Ben Hogan: 64

Arnold Palmer: 62

Byron Nelson: 52

Billy Casper: 51

Walter Hagen: 44

Cary Middlecoff: 40

Gene Sarazen: 39

Horton Smith: 32

Harry Cooper: 31

Leo Diegel: 30

Lee Trevino: 29

Henry Picard: 26

Johnny Miller: 25

Gary Player: 24

Vijay Singh: 23

Ray Floyd: 22

Lanny Wadkins: 21

Greg Norman: 20

THE COURSES
Where the Going Gets Rough

**A good golf course makes you want to play so badly
that you hardly have the time to change your shoes.**

– BEN CRENSHAW –

1

Which of the four major championships
is held at the same course each year?
A) The Masters   B) U.S. Open
C) British Open   D) PGA Championship

2

How many PGA TOUR events were hosted on
Tournament Players Club courses in 2004?

3

How many different courses are
played each year during the
Bob Hope Chrysler Classic?
A) One   B) Two
C) Three   D) Four

4

What course has
the Bank of America
Colonial been played on
since its inception in 1946?

1. *A) The Masters has been held at the Augusta National Golf Club since its inception in 1934.*

2. *10 events: FBR Open, THE PLAYERS Championship, BellSouth Classic, EDS Byron Nelson Championship, FedEx St. Jude Classic, Booz Allen Classic, John Deere Classic, Buick Championship, Deutsche Bank Championship, and the Michelin Championship at Las Vegas*

3. *D) Four*

4. *The Colonial Country Club in Fort Worth, Texas*

5

Which two golf courses have most
often played host to the U.S. Open?
A) Baltusrol and Oakmont
B) Baltusrol and Winged Foot
C) Olympia Fields and Inverness
D) Oakmont and Oakland Hills

6

The first time the U.S. Open was played
at a truly public course was in 2002.
What was the course?

7

Which was the shortest course
to ever hold the U.S. Open?
A) Newport Golf Club
B) The Country Club at Brookline
C) Shinnecock Hills
D) Brae Burn

8

What two courses share the record for being
the longest to play host to the U.S. Open?

5 **A) Baltusrol and Oakmont at seven times each**

6 **The Black Course at Bethpage State Park in Farmingdale, New York**

7 **C) Shinnecock Hills. It was just 4,423 yards when it held the 1896 tournament.**

8 **The Black Course at Bethpage State Park and Pinehurst No. 2, which both measure 7,214 yards. They held the U.S. Open in 2002 and 2005 respectively.**

From 1896 to 1914, Harry Vardon won a record six British Open titles. On which course did he win most of those?
A) Muirfield   B) St. Andrews
C) Prestwick   D) Royal St. Georges

THE PLAYERS Championship, the PGA TOUR's flagship event, moved to the Tournament Players Club at Sawgrass in 1982. How many courses played host to the event prior to that?

11

Tom Watson dominated the British Open between 1975 and 1983. On what course was he initially unable to defend his title?
A) Carnoustie
B) Turnberry
C) Royal Troon
D) Royal Birkdale

12

Which course has hosted the greatest number of British Opens?

9 *C) Prestwick. Vardon won four of his six titles there, including his final one in 1914, where, in an incredible comeback, he defeated J. H. Taylor by three strokes and at age 44 became the oldest man to put his name on the Claret Jug.*

10 *Four: Atlanta Country Club, Colonial Country Club, Inverrary Golf & Country Club, and Sawgrass Country Club*

11 *D) Royal Birkdale. Watson missed the cut there in 1976 as defending champion, but won his fifth and final British Open on that same course in 1983, this time successfully defending his title.*

12 *St. Andrews. The tournament was played there for the 27th time in 2005.*

18

13 ▶

The Michelin Championship at Las Vegas uses a
three-course rotation. Which of the following Tournament
Players Club courses is not used in that event?
A) TPC at Summerlin   B) TPC at The Canyons
C) TPC at River's Bend   D) None of the above

14 ▶

Which of the following was the first in the
Tournament Players Club network?
A) TPC at Deere Run   B) TPC at Sugarloaf
C) TPC at Sawgrass   D) TPC at Avenel

15 ▶

The 17th hole at the
Tournament Players Club at
Sawgrass is one of the most
famous in all of golf. At what length
is it most commonly played?
A) 110–119 yards   B) 120–129 yards
C) 130–139 yards   D) 140–149 yards

16 ▶

What is the nickname
of the eighth hole
at Royal Troon?

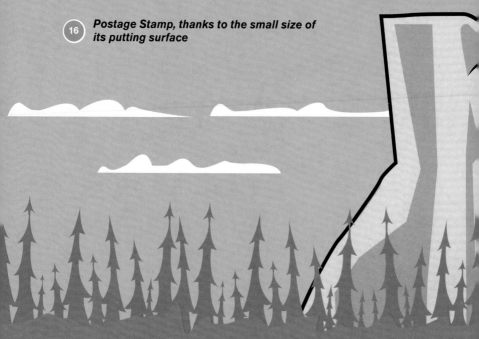

13 *C) TPC at River's Bend*

14 *C) TPC at Sawgrass*

15 *C) 130–139 yards*

16 *Postage Stamp, thanks to the small size of its putting surface*

17 ▸

Where were the first seven
PGA TOUR National Qualifying
Tournaments held?

18 ▸

Where was the first
Ryder Cup contested?

19 ▸

As of 2004, what was the only course other
than La Costa Resort and Spa to play host to
the World Golf Championships–Accenture
Match Play Championship?

20 ▸

What is the only course
to have hosted a
Presidents Cup competition
in the United States?

17 *PGA National Golf Club in Palm Beach Gardens, Florida*

18 *At the Worcester Country Club in Massachusetts*

19 *The Metropolitan Club in Victoria, Australia, which hosted the event in 2001*

20 *Robert Trent Jones Golf Club in Gainesville, Virginia*

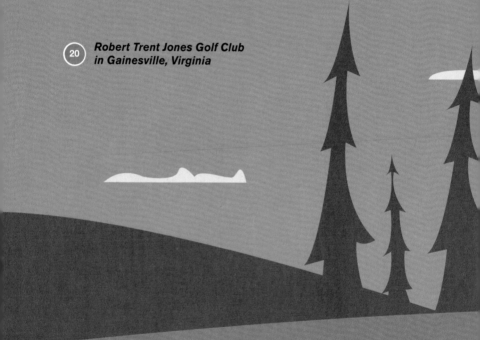

21
What golf course was played twice in 2004
during PGA TOUR–sanctioned events?
A) Valhalla Golf Club   B) Bellerive Country Club
C) Pebble Beach Golf Links   D) Both B and C

22
When was the last time Cypress
Point was used in the AT&T Pebble
Beach National Pro-Am?
A) 1990   B) 1991
C) 1996   D) 1997

23
On what course did Tiger
Woods play his first PGA TOUR
event as an amateur in 1992?

24
On which famed course did Tiger Woods
complete the career Grand Slam in 2000?
A) Augusta National   B) Pebble Beach
C) St. Andrews   D) Valhalla

21 *C) Pebble Beach Golf Links, which was the site of the PGA TOUR's AT&T Pebble Beach National Pro-Am and the Champions Tour's First Tee Open*

22 *A) 1990. Cypress Point, which had hosted the tournament every year since 1947, was replaced by Poppy Hills Golf Club in 1991.*

23 *Riviera Country Club, which played host to the Nissan Open*

24 *C) St. Andrews*

25

What golf course was the site of Jack Nicklaus's first PGA TOUR victory?

26

What historic golf course features holes named Bobby Jones and Tom Morris?

27

Which of the following was Bobby Jones's home course?
A) Atlanta Athletic Club   B) East Lake Golf Club
C) Georgia Country Club   D) Peachtree Golf Club

28

Where did Bobby Jones play in his first U.S. Amateur?

25. *The Oakmont Country Club, where Nicklaus won the 1962 U.S. Open*

26. *The Old Course in St. Andrews, Scotland*

27. *B) East Lake Golf Club in Atlanta, Georgia*

28. *Merion Cricket Club in Ardmore, Pennsylvania, in 1916*

29

Jack Nicklaus and Arnold Palmer have individually designed hundreds of courses. Name the only course that the two legends worked on together.

30

Approximately how many golf courses is Robert Trent Jones Sr. credited with designing or redesigning?

31

Which golf course is not a Robert Trent Jones Sr. design?
A) Bellerive   B) Whistling Straits
C) Hazeltine D) Firestone

32

Who does famed golf course architect Pete Dye credit with the idea of making the famous 17th hole at the Tournament Players Club at Sawgrass an island hole?

29 *The King and Bear, located in St. Augustine, Florida*

30 *About 500 courses*

31 *B) Whistling Straits*

32 *His wife, Alice*

A

I was home to the first 12 British Opens and saw "Old" Tom Morris and "Young" Tom Morris win eight times during that span. I hosted my 24th and final British Open in 1925. After that point, I was deemed too small and restrictive for the burgeoning sport. What course am I?

B

My first six holes were laid out in 1893, and the great Willie Campbell added three holes a year later. By 1899 I had a full 18 holes. Since then I have seen some of golf's greatest victories, including Francis Ouimet's stunning U.S. Open victory in 1913 and Justin Leonard's amazing 45-foot putt on No. 17, which allowed the U.S. to win the Ryder Cup in 1999. What course am I?

C

I was designed by the legendary Donald Ross, and my first professional was Walter Hagen. Ben Hogan called me a monster after he won the U.S. Open on me in 1951. I hosted my 10th major championship in 1996 and was home to the 35th Ryder Cup in 2004. What course am I?

D

The Roaring 1920s brought the biggest golfers and movie stars of the day out to play on me. I first played host to the Nissan Open in 1929 and have hosted it annually since 1973. One of my most unusual features is a bunker in the middle of the green at No. 6. What course am I?

E

I was built on the site of what was formerly the Fruitland Nurseries. All 18 of my holes have colorful names, such as Pink Dogwood, Flowering Peach, and Camellia. I also host one of golf's most historic tournaments each April. What course am I?

WHAT COURSE AM I?

A Prestwick Golf Club in Ayrshire, Scotland

B The Country Club in Brookline, Massachusetts

C Oakland Hills Country Club in Bloomfield Hills, Michigan

D The Riviera Country Club in Pacific Palisades, California

E Augusta National in Augusta, Georgia

33 ▶

Which of the courses below is
not an Alister Mackenzie design?
A) Augusta National
B) Cypress Point
C) Royal Melbourne
D) Pinehurst No. 2

34 ▶

How many courses comprise Pinehurst
Resort and Country Club in North Carolina?

35 ▶

Which of the many
courses at Pinehurst goes
by a name and a number?

36 ▶

Which two World
Golf Hall of Fame
members inspired
the name of
The Slammer &
The Squire course
at World Golf Village?

33 *D) Pinehurst No. 2*

34 *Eight*

35 *No. 8, which opened in 1996 to commemorate Pinehurst's centennial year and is also known as Centennial*

36 *Sam Snead and Gene Sarazen*

37

How did the English Turn Golf & Country Club get its name?

38

On what course is the oldest first tee in continuous use in the United States?

39

What is the only golf course on the PGA TOUR that annually plays as a par 73?
A) Redstone Golf Club   B) The Plantation Course
C) Castle Pines   D) Forest Oaks Country Club

40

What golf course is known as Hogan's Alley?

41

Which course has never seen a competitive round of 59 shot during a PGA TOUR event?
A) Colonial Country Club in Memphis
B) Sunrise Golf Club
C) Westchester Country Club
D) The Palmer Course at PGA West

37 *The name can be traced to an event in 1699, when a French exploration party turned back an English warship floating down the lower Mississippi River.*

38 *The Old Course at The Homestead in Hot Springs, Virginia. It dates back to 1892.*

39 *B) The Plantation Course in Hawaii, the site of the Mercedes Championships*

40 *Colonial Country Club in Fort Worth, Texas. Ben Hogan, a native Texan, mastered the course like no other. He won the first two tournaments there in 1946 and 1947, then won again in 1952, 1953, and 1959.*

41 *C) Westchester Country Club*

42

Which PGA TOUR course plays its 18th hole into the shadows of a lighthouse?

43

What is a links course?

44

How do golfers measure the speed of greens on a golf course?

45

What is often called the "19th hole" on a golf course?

46

How many balls annually are hit in the water at No. 17 at the Tournament Players Club at Sawgrass?
A) 100,000   B) 150,000
C) 200,000   D) 250,000

42 Harbour Town Golf Links on Hilton Head Island, site of the MCI Classic

43 In its purest sense, a links course is one built between a seaside area and an area more suitable for cultivation. In essence, the land where the course is built—where it is nearly impossible to cultivate vegetation and tree growth—links the beach to the land with agricultural capability.

44 With a Stimpmeter, a V-shaped device that supports a golf ball. When the Stimpmeter is lowered to approximately 20 degrees, the ball rolls down the device, accelerating at six feet per second. The distance that the ball travels on the putting surface is the stimp speed. (For example, a stimp of 11 indicates the ball rolled 11 feet.)

45 The bar in the clubhouse

46 B) 150,000—an average of more than three per person

BUNKER SHOT

MATCH THESE COURSES ON THE 2004 PGA TOUR
SCHEDULE TO THE TOURNAMENT THAT WAS PLAYED THERE:

The Plantation Course	Wachovia Championship
Tournament Players Club of Scottsdale	B.C. Open
TPC at Sawgrass (Stadium Course)	THE TOUR Championship Presented by Coca-Cola
TPC at Sugarloaf	Bell Canadian Open
Redstone Golf Club	FBR Open
Quail Hollow Golf Club	Mercedes Championships
TPC at Southwind	World Golf Championships–American Express Championship
Westchester Country Club	Buick Open
TPC at Avenel	Buick Championship
En-Joie Golf Club	Shell Houston Open
Warwick Hills Golf & Country Club	Buick Classic
Castle Pines Golf Club	Chrysler Classic of Greensboro
Firestone Country Club (South Course)	FedEx St. Jude Classic
Montreux Golf & Country Club	The INTERNATIONAL
TPC at River Highlands	Booz Allen Classic
Glen Abbey Golf Club	BellSouth Classic
Mount Juliet Estate	World Golf Championships–NEC Invitational
Annandale Golf Club	Reno-Tahoe Open
Forest Oaks Country Club	Southern Farm Bureau Classic
East Lake Golf Club	THE PLAYERS Championship

BUNKER SHOT

ANSWERS:

The Plantation Course: Mercedes Championships

Tournament Players Club of Scottsdale: FBR Open

TPC at Sawgrass (Stadium Course): THE PLAYERS Championship

TPC at Sugarloaf: BellSouth Classic

Redstone Golf Club: Shell Houston Open

Quail Hollow Club: Wachovia Championship

TPC at Southwind: FedEx St. Jude Classic

Westchester Country Club: Buick Classic

TPC at Avenel: Booz Allen Classic

En-Joie Golf Club: B.C. Open

Warwick Hills Golf & Country Club: Buick Open

Castle Pines Golf Club: The INTERNATIONAL

**Firestone Country Club (South Course): World Golf
Championships-NEC Invitational**

Montreux Golf & Country Club: Reno-Tahoe Open

TPC at River Highlands: Buick Championship

Glen Abbey Golf Club: Bell Canadian Open

**Mount Juliet Estate: World Golf Championships-
American Express Championship**

Annandale Golf Club: Southern Farm Bureau Classic

Forest Oaks Country Club: Chrysler Classic of Greensboro

**East Lake Golf Club: THE TOUR Championship
presented by Coca-Cola**

PLAYERS INDEX

MARK CUBBEDGE is the communications manager for the World Golf Hall of Fame in his native St. Augustine, Florida. He oversees the annual ballot process for the Hall of Fame and as a member of its exhibit team, has helped develop comprehensive Arnold Palmer and Bobby Jones exhibits, among others. Previously he spent nearly six years covering golf for PGATOUR.COM. He won't disclose his golf handicap but says his trivia handicap is nearly scratch–further proof that simply knowing a lot about golf won't help you on the first tee.

He dedicates this book to his grandparents, who would have been first in line at the bookstore; to Andy Clayton, who in his zest for golf would have started a one-man promotions team; and most importantly, to his wife, Nicole, whose faith and love–and patience during his "research" on the greens–remain an eternal blessing.